Praise For IF/THEN

I've been a fan of both Rusty and Michael for years, so I opened this book with great anticipation. A short time later, I closed the book with great appreciation. Thoroughly Biblical and an engaging read, If/Then encouraged, challenged and equipped me to better follow Christ. This little guide will help you partner in God's "very great and precious promises" (2 Peter 1:4), and I promise you: If you'll read this book seriously, then God will seriously bless you!

MATT PROCTOR, PRESIDENT, OZARK CHRISTIAN COLLEGE

Rusty and Michael powerfully and practically will help you revaluate your relationship with God from the ground up. One of the most important things to figure out in any relationship is which role each person is going to fulfill. It's no different in our relationship with God. We tend to focus on the role He promises to fulfill, and that's certainly important information we need to know. But we also need to know what His expectations are for us in this relationship. Here's the beautiful thing this book celebrates—God always keeps His promises. So if we choose to participate in this relationship, then we know He'll hold up His end of it.

KYLE IDLEMAN, TEACHING PASTOR, SOUTHEAST CHRISTIAN CHURCH, AUTHOR OF NOT A FAN AND GODS AT WAR

If you believe Jesus calls you to be a disciple, but struggle how to become a disciple, this book is for you. Rusty George has given every follower of Jesus a vital tool for spiritual transformation.

GENE APPEL, SENIOR PASTOR, EASTSIDE CHRISTIAN CHURCH

My friends, Rusty and Michael both write in such a way that you just know that they unconditionally trust the promises of God. And both of them actually live that way! I'm confident that IF you will soak in the words of this book, THEN you will experience significant growth in your understanding of the God who loves you.

MIKE BREAUX, TEACHING PASTOR, HEARTLAND COMMUNITY CHURCH

If/Then

If/Then

Unleashing God's Power in Your Life

Rusty George

and

Michael DeFazio

If/Then. Copyright ©2013 by Rusty George and Michael DeFazio.

All rights reserved. Printed in the United States of America. No part of this book may be used or reproduced in any manner whatsoever without written permission except in the case of brief quotations embodied in critical articles and reviews.

Published by Real Life Church (reallifechurch.org) in association with Samizdat Creative, a division of Samizdat Publishing Group, LLC (samizdatcreative.com).

ISBN: 978-1-938633-35-5
ebook ISBN: 978-1-938633-36-2

Unless otherwise noted, all Scripture references use the *New International Version*.

Contents

Preface ... 3

Week 1: I Surrender / He Saves

Day 1: If we confess him as Lord ... 13
Day 2: If we are baptized ... 17
Day 3: If we repent ... 23
Day 4: If we confess ... 29

Week 2: I Seek / He Reveals

Day 1: If we look at Jesus ... 37
Day 2: If we listen to the ways God speaks ... 43
Day 3: If we seek God above all else ... 49
Day 4: If we love one another ... 55

Week 3: I Remain / He Produces

Day 1: If we put sin to death ... 67
Day 2: If we meditate on God's words ... 73
Day 3: If we ask God for wisdom ... 79
Day 4: If we pay attention to God's presence and power ... 85

Week 4: I Obey / He Blesses

Day 1: If we let our light shine	99
Day 2: If we honor me	105
Day 3: If we practice purity	111
Day 4: If we seek him first	117

Week 5: I Serve / He Multiplies

Day 1: If we invest our finances in the mission	127
Day 2: If we exercise our spiritual gifts	135
Day 3: If we tell people about Jesus	145
Day 4: If we endure suffering	153

Epilogue   161

*Dedicated to the people of Real Life Church.
We are so grateful God has allowed us to be part of
what he is doing in you.*

Preface

Some time ago I began attending a pastors conference in Dallas, Texas. What most may think would be the most boring week ever, I actually find rather exciting. Two days of conversation with other church leaders about strategies, messages, and creative ways to help people connect with Jesus is always invigorating to me. After a full day of intense discussion, we retreated to a local restaurant for dinner. Somewhere between the salad and the steak, we began sharing great life-change stories. This was one of the highlights of the trip for me. Hearing how God has changed people's lives is always a thrill. I shared a couple, some others shared theirs, and then a pastor from North Carolina spoke up.

He began to tell the story of a woman in his community who had run pretty far from God, and then was invited to their church. She showed up reluctantly at first, but she kept coming back. She got involved and eventually gave her life to Christ. It wasn't long after this that her pre-Christian struggles returned, though. She slipped back into her old ways of thinking and behaving and found herself wondering, *What good is this Christianity stuff anyway?* Finally, she sat down with her pastor and explained her feeling of buyer's remorse. After listening to her story, this pastor said words to her I pray she never forgets: "God has a great plan for your life, but you're going to have to participate!"

This phrase struck a chord with me. For the last few years I'd been feeling this overwhelming tension. We see people far from God take steps toward him, they start coming to church, they even get a Bible, they pray a prayer, they get baptized, and then about six months later they say, "Hey, why do I still have the same struggles? I prayed a prayer, even took a baptistery bath, so why isn't everything magically fixed?" They begin to wonder if they did something wrong, or maybe God just isn't holding up his end of the bargain.

In other words, *whose responsibility is it for life to change?*

Preface

The common assumption is: "It's God's!"

He's supposed to take away all temptation, shore up our weaknesses, remove our doubts, heal our sicknesses, and clear our paths to all financial, emotional, physical, and vocational success. So when he hasn't, does that mean there is no God? Or worse yet, that he's not all that great?

Here's another assumption: "It's mine."

We need to pray longer, study deeper, watch less TV, be in the church every time the doors are open, give ninety percent and live on ten. Then our lives will radically change and we'll find the life we've been seeking. And as long as we think our life isn't what we think it should be, we beat ourselves up over it and assume it's because we're just as worthless to God as we think we are to others.

A final assumption we make is: "It's the Church's."

If the pastor would just yell more, scold more, or educate more, then he'd preach the sin right out of us. Or if the church would just offer a few more programs or a few more studies, then we'd all immediately turn into the picture of perfection God had in mind when he created us. But if education were the issue, I guess Satan would be a great disciple. He knows more than all of us. While education is needed, it's bigger than that. And if busyness and serving were the only issue, then Jesus wouldn't have corrected Martha for working when she could have just spent time with him. When we assume that it's the church's responsibility to do everything for us, we'll always be "church shopping." But no place will ever be enough, because it was never intended to be enough.

The words this pastor spoke that day struck a chord with me because it reminded me of something we often forget. And that is being a part of the Kingdom of God, our spiritual journey, is all about a partnership with God. It's not a solo act.

Paul says it this way in Philippians:

> *Continue to work out your salvation with fear and trembling, for it is God who works in you to will and to act in order to fulfill to his good purpose. (Phil 2:12-13)*

In other words, I have my part; he has his. It's not

just his responsibility, or *only* mine, or even *all* on the church, it's a partnership. God has a plan for our lives, but we have to participate.

While the Bible makes it clear that there is only one way to God—that being Jesus—and that it is his free gift of grace that brings us back to God, it also makes it clear that once we are there, we live in partnership with God. And while we stand in grace, we live by faith. James says, "Faith without deeds is dead" (2.26). In other words, Jesus has saved us, but for a purpose. Not just for a get out of hell free card.

Throughout the Bible there are what we would call "If/Then" statements: "If you do this, then God will do this." It was the way God established his relationship with his people in the Old Testament. They were already his people, but there was a way he wanted them to behave as his people so that his partnership would make the maximum impact in their lives and in the world. And the same is true today. God still has If/Then statements that, when we decide to apply them, we are more than just educated, more than just obedient—we live in participation with God's great plan for our lives and the world.

This book is a journey through some of these If/Then statements that have the potential to unleash God's power in your life. Up till now, you may have been operating on your own strength or just expecting him to do everything for you, but this book will draw your attention to when God has said, "I've got this," and when he tells us, "This is all you need to do. If you do it, you'll discover my plan for your life. Simply by participating, you can unleash my promises in your life."

Week 1

I Surrender
He Saves

Most of us assume that being a Christian is about doing things. So, when we talk about If/Then statements our first reaction is, *Sure, I get that: If I behave myself, God will love me. If I do a lot of good deeds, God might even bless me. And if I clean up my act, conquer my addiction, serve the poor and give a lot of money, then maybe God will let me into heaven.* That's why if we were asked, "If you died tonight, would you go to heaven?" most of us would answer, "I think so." Because we just aren't confident that we've done enough.

But when you look at how Jesus interacted with people, he didn't seem to emphasize lists very much. In fact, the one thing that Jesus seemed most interested in was relationships. God, in human form, was much more concerned about us having a friendship with him than with how good we are when we meet him.

Take a look at this story Matthew tells us about his own "come to Jesus" meeting. What you need to understand about this is that Matthew was a tax collector. And as much as we might not enjoy the IRS today, in those days tax collectors were seen as so unscrupulous, so underhanded, and so socially repulsive, they would be compared to that slimy character behind the school selling drugs to seventh graders. People couldn't stand tax collectors. And yet, Jesus invites one into his inner circle.

As Jesus was walking along, he saw a man named Matthew sitting at his tax collector's booth. "Follow me and be my disciple," Jesus said to him. So Matthew got up and followed him. Later, Matthew invited Jesus and his disciples to his home as dinner guests, along with many tax collectors and other disreputable sinners. But when the Pharisees saw this, they asked his disciples, "Why does your teacher eat with such scum?" When Jesus heard this, he said, "Healthy people don't need a doctor—sick people do." (Matt 9:9-12 NLT)

Here's what's so interesting about this: The Pharisees were the ones who were very successful at what we would consider to be God-honoring, good behavior. They were the ones you'd think would have Jesus' attention. But instead, it's the morally reprehensible that Jesus had dinner with. That's because the issue isn't about our spiritual success, but rather our spiritual surrender. The one thing the Pharisees wouldn't do that Matthew did . . . was follow Jesus.

We tend to think, *If I change/then I can follow.*

Jesus says, "If you follow me/then I'll change you."

As we start week one, the most important way we begin participation with God is in our salvation process. When it comes to the If/Then statements involving our coming to Jesus, it doesn't start with what we do. It starts with who we know.

When it comes to our salvation, all our If/Then assumptions are about our successes—if I succeed at being good, then I'll be saved. But Jesus says it's all about surrender. *Follow me. Surrender to me. And not only will you begin to change, I'll help you do what you could never do on your own.*

Over the course of this week, we'll walk through four major points of surrender and see how God does incredible things in our lives as we begin to not just follow, but surrender to him.

For a deeper look at this content and to actually see/hear this message brought 'to life' in front of the congregation at Real Life Church, please go to www.reallifechurch.org/ifthen/week1.

Day 1

If we confess him as Lord
Then we will be saved

Pastoring a church in the Los Angeles area can have its benefits. Occasionally some generous individual will give me a ticket to a Lakers game. There is nothing quite like the thrill of seeing NBA basketball up close and personal. The beauty of the game, the gracefulness of the players, the roar of the crowd, all combine for an amazing evening. But in order to experience it, you have to get in the building.

There have been many times when the ticket I'm receiving has been left for me at the will call window at the arena. I have to walk up, say my name, and then tell them the name of the person who left the ticket.

"I'm here to pick up a ticket. It's under the name of . . ." It's in this moment that I am completely at the mercy of the one who left me the ticket. I can't buy a ticket—the game is sold out. I can't sneak my way in—plenty of security. The only way in is by the ticket provided for me. I'm at the mercy of the giver . . . and I surrender to their way of getting me into the stadium.

Following Jesus, though a much greater situation, is similar. In Romans 10, Paul reminds the reader that up until the moment Jesus arrived, the people of God felt that their standing with him was based on their performance for him. And because of this, they had begun to place their trust in their own goodness, to the point that many felt their righteousness would earn them a spot in heaven. In other words, they were trying to purchase their own ticket. Paul, the author of this passage, once held this line of thinking. But when he was confronted by Jesus and convicted of his sin, he soon discovered the only thing that makes us right before God is Jesus himself.

> *That if you confess with your mouth, "Jesus is Lord," and believe in your heart that God raised him from the dead, you will be saved. (Rom 10:9)*

Then, just four verses later he says,

> "Everyone who calls on the name of the Lord will be saved." (Rom 10:13)

Paul is saying that surrendering to Jesus begins by placing our trust in him as our only way into his kingdom.

Just as much as I do nothing more to get into the Lakers game than put my trust in the one who gave me the ticket and simply receive their gracious gift, so it is when I come to faith in Christ. It doesn't start by my perfection or good deeds any more than my getting in the game is based on how well I dress or how much money I tip the will call attendant. It all comes down to whose name I trust to get me in. And believing in Jesus and confessing his name is just that—I put my trust in him, believing that he's the only way I'm getting into the kingdom of God.

I've seen us trust a lot of other names.

A favorite is to trust in the name of family members: *My dad was a pastor,* or *My grandmother prayed for me every day,* or *I grew up in a Christian home.* This is placing your trust in someone else who has placed their trust in Jesus, rather than doing it yourself.

Another common name we trust is our own. *I'll get there by my abilities. I'm a good person. Surely God will let me in. I'm better than my friends.* But simply being better than another isn't trust in the one who was perfect.

Just like the Lakers game for me . . . it's not complicated. It's not even all that difficult. It's about showing up and admitting that the only way I'm getting in is by the grace of someone else. Just like the kingdom of God.

So here's my question: Whose name are you hoping "gets you in?"

If you go with Jesus / Then you get salvation.

Day 2

If we are baptized
Then we will receive the Holy Spirit

I am not a golfer. Everyone expects me to be since I'm a middle-aged pastor. You'd think it's some sort of prerequisite. So, I get invited to play, but usually decline because it'd be embarrassing for all involved. But once a year, I go out with a foursome to play in a golf scramble that benefits one of the non-profits we support. It's usually at this event that I'm reminded of this simple fact: I am not a golfer.

This is the way a lot of us feel when we think about following Jesus. We haven't been to church much, the only part of the Bible we've read is the cover, and we only pray when we take a test, get pulled over by a cop, or perhaps when we golf. And because of our feelings of inadequacy, we think, *I could never be a follower of Jesus.*

Unfortunately, this feeling of being in "deep weeds" doesn't just happen when we go to church, it happens in everyday life. We struggle with addictions, we try to suppress our anger, we try to hide our deepest struggles. Things like: We love our family, we just don't like them sometimes. We smile when our neighbor brings home a new boat, but inside we're consumed with jealousy. We act like we have it together, but we fear we'll one day be exposed for being a complete fraud. So, every now and then we think, *I've got to get this together.* Or, we go to church and hear, "Jesus has a better way for you to live," and we think, *I'd like that, but I just can't do it. I could never be a follower of Jesus.*

In the book of Acts, we read about the events that happened about three months after Jesus' crucifixion and resurrection. One of Jesus' closest followers, Peter, stands up before thousands of people and cuts to the chase: "Hey, this Jesus that you killed? He's the Son of God! You've been looking for the Messiah, and you missed him." And for the first time the people have the great "Aha!" moment and get it! They wonder how they can make this right, and Peter gives them one of the great If/Then statements of our faith.

> *Peter replied, "Repent and be baptized, every one of you, in the name of Jesus Christ for the forgiveness of your sins. And you will receive the gift of the Holy Spirit. (Acts 2:38)*

He says, "repent," which means to turn from your current way of doing life. He says, "be baptized," which means to symbolize your commitment to Jesus by being immersed in water. And then not only will you be forgiven, but you'll also receive the Holy Spirit.

In other words, *if* we choose to follow him, if we choose to submit to him through this symbol of being buried and resurrected through the watery grave of baptism, *then* not only will forgiveness be applied to our accounts, but we'll also be given the gift of the very Spirit of God in our lives.

Most of us stop when we hear about forgiveness. Who wouldn't want that? Having my record cleared? Having my debts paid? Off the hook for all the wrong

I've done? Count me in. Dunk me now! But the hidden treasure in this If/Then statement is the gift of the Holy Spirit.

All through the Bible we read that God is constantly getting closer to us. At first he's a voice from beyond the clouds, then a pillar of fire and cloud, then in the Ark of the Covenant, then in a temple, and then he gets so close that he's human—Jesus! But God says, "I'll get even closer. I'll move right into your life and I'll bring all my transformation power and begin to change you from the inside out! That will be my very Holy Spirit living inside of you."

Back to my horrible golf game. Recently, my once a year golf date was here. I had to find three other golfers to help offset my inadequacies. So, I recruited a professional golfer from our church. I thought between he and I, our game should balance out to about average. But just the opposite happened. Because I was with greatness, I got better. Sometimes he made up for my mistakes, but sometimes he corrected the mistakes I was making. And by the end of the day, I was a better golfer. When greatness took a seat in my cart, it changed my game.

The beauty of God's offering to us is this: When we surrender to him in baptism, he takes up residence in our cart, in our lives, and it will change your game. The Bible tells us what this looks like by giving us the "fruit," or the result, of the Spirit in our lives—things like love, joy, peace, patience, kindness, goodness, gentleness, self-control, faithfulness. In other words, the person you've always wanted to be, the person your spouse is hoping you'll become, the person your kids deserve to have as a parent, the person God created you to be—it is possible. Not because of your trying, but because of his training.

If we are baptized into Him / Then we will receive the Holy Spirit.

I think all of us could use that kind of greatness moving into our lives.

Day 3

If we repent
Then we will find refreshment

Ever miss your exit? You've been driving in a new city and you're already a bit confused. It's getting dark, you're trying to reach your destination and, even though you've got GPS on your phone, let's be honest—you wonder if that sweet voice behind that app really knows what she's talking about. And then you miss your exit. And the voice on the phone says, "Recalculating." In other words, "You're an idiot and now I've got to find a way to fix your mistake." Maybe it's just me who hears that.

There's a feeling you have when you are off course. You know you're not going where you should, you know you're not going to reach your destination this way, and you just feel unsettled. But then you find that next exit and you turn around and the moment you get back on the highway you feel this sense of peace. Not because you've arrived, not because you even know exactly where you are going, but because at least you know you're going the right direction.

God offers this same kind of confidence. You may not know all the details of the destination, but you can have the peace that comes from knowing you are going in the right direction. Peter says these words in Acts 3:

> *Repent, then, and turn to God, so that your sins may be wiped out, that times of refreshing may come from the Lord. (Acts 3:19)*

There's that word again: repent.

Repentance means a turning around. Much like your experience on that lonely highway when you've driven way past your exit, there comes a moment you need to turn the car around and go in another direction. In this case, repentance is the moment you say, "My ideas, my theories, my gut, my way of living has only taken me off course and in a direction different than where God would have me. So, it's time to turn it around. It's time to repent."

All of us have a map we've been using to get through life: It may be what our parents taught us, it may be what we've experienced, it may just be our feelings, but we've got our map. And though some of these things may be good, some may be wise, some may even be right, they all have one fundamental flaw: You're in charge. You're the one calling the shots. You're the one writing your own laws, your own code, your own way of doing things.

But when you realize you've missed your exit—when you realize your map has lead you into a marriage filled with conflict, friendships that are shallow, kids that are distant, a job that is unfulfilling, and there's not much hope for the future, you have to stop and realize that you are not always the best map maker.

Repentance is done in a moment—and lived for a lifetime.

It begins when you say: "God, I'm lost. My way has only led me to confusion, conflict, and distance from those I love. I want to turn around and go your way."

The tricky thing is that it means we surrender the map making to him. And even though we don't always know what "recalculating" will mean, we trust that he knows better than us. After all, he created us and he can see things from a better vantage point than we have.

My wife called me one day and said, "I'm lost." I said, "Are you using your phone GPS?" She said, "No, can you guide me?" So I used an app on my phone that allowed me to see exactly where she was and where she was headed. I was then able to give her turn-by-turn directions that helped her get back on course. And the reason I could do this? I was seeing things from a satellite view; she was seeing things from a street view. I had a better vantage point than her.

Something happens when we surrender to the one with a better vantage point. It's the same thing that happens when we turn the car around and get back going in the right direction: peace. The phrase that this verse uses is, "times of refreshing will come" (NLT).

The great thing is the promise in this verse: *if we repent, then times of refreshing will come.*

We may not know the next turn, but we know someone who does. And as we follow him, rather than going our own way, we find peace.

Day 4

If we confess
Then we will be forgiven

We talked about confession earlier in this book, but that was the concept of confessing the name of Christ as our Lord and Savior, the leader and forgiver of our lives. But confession is a practice that can do even more than just announce the name of the one we follow. Today's If/Then statement can bring a freedom like you've never experienced.

When my youngest daughter Sidney was about two-years-old, she began the practice of confession. My wife walked into our laundry room only to find clothes strewn about in a disheveled mess. She looked at our two daughters and said, "Who did this?" Sidney, knowing she'd been caught, looked down at the floor and then confessed, "I did it. And I did it on purpose." There was something freeing about saying, with determination, that she did it.

I'd say that it's easier for a two-year-old to come clean than a twenty-year-old, or a forty-year-old. Something happens as we get older. We get calloused, we get used to carrying a burden, and we learn to conceal a secret. Eventually, we just learn how to live with our sin. I have a friend who is a marriage and family therapist and he always reminds people of the sage wisdom: it's our secrets that make us sick.

John points us in this direction, and this is where our If/Then statement comes from today:

> *If we confess our sins, he is faithful and just and will forgive us our sins and purify us from all unrighteousness. (1 John 1:9)*

If we confess / *then* he forgives.

He doesn't even specify that we need to beg for forgiveness, or promise to never do it again. He simply says, "Confess." When we decide to verbalize our sins, he forgives and cleanses us from the stain of our sin. That's it. The burden is lifted.

But this principle doesn't just come into effect through our relationship with God—it can even bring great results through our relationships with others.

Look what James, the half-brother of Jesus, writes:

> *Therefore confess your sins to each other and pray for each other so that you may be healed. The prayer of a righteous person is powerful and effective. (Jas 5:16)*

Confessing our sins in private is one thing, and it brings a clean slate with God. But when we go so far as to confess our sins to a trusted friend—that brings healing.

I recently had someone come up to me and ask, "Can I just tell God? Do I have to really tell someone else?" I said, "Well, you can do that, but you'll limit your healing." While confession to God alone can bring forgiveness—and it's enough—the thing that seems to break the sin streak and limit the power of guilt is when we decide to bring someone else into our pain.

I've counseled people who have kept secrets for years about something they did or something they are currently doing. And the moment I hear those words, "I'm going to tell you something I've never told anyone," I get excited. Not because I'm getting to hear their dirt, but because I know that a weight is about to be lifted. As soon as they say it, it's like someone just drove a truck off of their shoulders.

For many Christ-followers, we've surrendered. We've confessed Jesus as Lord, we've been baptized, we are even practicing repentance. But we still feel stuck in a sin cycle we can't escape. That's because we've forgotten this final principle of confession to others. By bringing our sin into the light by sharing it with a trusted friend, we find healing.

Week 2

I Seek
He Reveals

Do you want to know God? Do you want to see God?

I want you to really think about those questions: Do I want to know God? Do I want God to reveal himself to me?

I don't just mean know *about* God, though we shouldn't downplay the importance of that, either. You can't know God personally without knowing true things about God, and often the pathway to a personal relationship begins by pursuing the truth *about* The One Behind It All.

But I'm talking about more than right information. I'm talking about encounter, about experience. Do you want to be one of those people who actually have *experiences* of God?

Most of us would say *yes* (at least most of us handling this book). But we probably shouldn't be so quick to answer! Think about the people who have had legitimate experiences of God in the Bible, and think about the outcome of those experiences.

Abraham was going about his business, probably not much different from all the other people living in his day and age. One day he hears from God—the God he didn't really even know was real, mind you. God suddenly speaks to him, and part of it is great because this great God is making promises to Abraham. He's making the kind of promises we all want to hear: "You're going to be great. You're going to have a huge and lasting family. You're going to have massive property to enjoy. You're going to have influence far beyond your years on earth. Matter of fact, everyone else who lives will be blessed because of your greatness and blessing." But there's a catch of sorts. God also says, "I want you to leave everything you've ever known. Leave your homeland, your stuff, your father's household." And as if that weren't drastic enough, God didn't even tell Abraham where he was going! Abraham was just supposed to start walking and assume he'd hear from God along the way.

That's borderline crazy!

Or take Moses. Here's a fugitive on the run hiding from his past who, like Abraham, was just going about his business. Then one day he spots a "burning bush." Now in the desert heat he was accustomed to, bushes spontaneously catching fire weren't all that uncommon. But this one keeps burning without being destroyed—and then God starts talking from it! And what he says is, "Go back to the place you ran away from and confront the most powerful man in the world with the news that he's about to lose most of his labor force."

Those are only *two* examples! Never mind the stories of Joshua and Samuel and David. We haven't even talked about Isaiah and Jeremiah and Hosea. And don't get me started on Mary, John, Paul, and Jesus.

So I ask you again: Do you want to know God? Do

you want God to come to you, show you who he is, talk to you? I hope you do, because the only right answer is yes. God may seem crazy, but knowing him is the sweetest, richest, most life-giving experience you will ever know. It is literally what you were made for.

So let's get to it. This week we're talking about doing the simple things God requires before he will reveal himself to us. Learn these things, start doing these things, and someday we'll get together and share stories about the unpredictable, borderline ridiculous, wild and crazy, world-changing things God says, does, and asks us to do.

For a deeper look at this content and to actually see/hear this message brought 'to life' in front of the congregation at Real Life Church, please go to www.reallifechurch.org/ifthen/week2.

Day 1

If we look at Jesus
Then we'll see God's face

A kindergarten teacher observed her classroom while the children drew pictures. She occasionally walked around to see each child's artwork, and as she approached one little girl who was working diligently, the teacher asked the girl what she was drawing.

"I'm drawing God," replied the little girl.

The teacher paused and said, "But sweetheart, no one knows what God looks like."

And without taking her eyes off the page, the girl answered, "They will when I'm done."

It's a cute story you've probably heard before, but it also raises some very important questions: What is God like? How do we know? Who can tell or show us? This week's topic—*if we seek God, then God reveals himself to us*—is great and all, but where are we supposed to look?

Most things can be found if you look hard enough or in the right places. For example, when we lose our car keys, we retrace our steps. Why? Because we assume that the keys must be someplace we have recently been. When we get lost heading to the store or someone's house, we plug our destination's address into an electronic device and follow the directions. Why? Because the map we're shown represents the most reliable way to get there.

Again, most things can be found if you look hard enough or in the right places. But other things can't simply be *found*. They must be *revealed*. Many times you cannot in your own power find out what your friend or spouse or child thinks about some issue or problem. They must *reveal* that information to us.

God falls into this second category. God is not someone you can understand by natural ability or hard work. You may be very bright, but even your genius has limits. God must reveal himself or God will forever remain unknown.

Thankfully, God is inclined to reveal.

Throughout the story of God and Israel in the Old Testament, God arrives on the scene in some interesting ways. He comes in a burning bush or a den of lions, through victories on a battlefield or poems written in a field, with the words of a prophet or the beauties of creation, through commands inscribed on stone tablets or an old widow's never-ending supply of oil. And that's just a small sampling.

But according to the New Testament, all these pale in comparison to the one place God has fully and finally revealed himself. This place is actually a person, and this person is Jesus. "In the past God spoke to our ancestors through the prophets at many times and in various ways," writes the author of Hebrews, "but in these last days he has spoken to us by his Son, whom he appointed heir of all things, and through whom also he made the universe." Then notice what comes next: "The Son is the radiance of God's glory and the exact representation of his being" (Heb 1.1-3).

Hebrews certainly isn't alone. Jesus' best friend put it this way: "No one has ever seen God, but the one and only Son, who is himself God and is in closest relationship with the Father, has made him known" (John 1.18). And Paul needed even fewer words to make the same point: "The Son is the image of the invisible God" (Col 1.15).

But none put it as simply as Jesus himself: "Anyone who has seen me has seen the Father" (John 14.9).

Technically, we're talking about *incarnation*. Jesus is the divine Son of God. Jesus is God fully taking on the form of a human person and entering our world so that we might know him in friendship and in truth. Incarnation accomplishes revelation. Jesus reveals to us what we otherwise would never know. More clearly than any other book or tradition or religion or person, Jesus reveals God.

Do you want to know how God responds to people caught in adultery? Do you want to hear what God thinks of religion? Do you want to see how God feels about poverty?

Do you want to know how God treats the people you hate? Do you want to hear what God says to outcasts and sinners? Do you want to see what God is doing about human suffering?

Do you want to know his justice? Do you want to hear his gentleness? Do you want to see his grace?

God has shown us who God is. God has revealed his identity and character. God has drawn us a picture of himself in his Son. If you want to discover God, look closely at Jesus.

Day 2

If we listen to the ways God speaks
Then we will hear his voice

About once every six months someone looks me square in the eye and asks if God talks to me.

The question comes from all different kinds of people: some who follow Jesus, some who are thinking about following Jesus, and some who think following Jesus is crazy. But no matter who it comes from, it's one of the most honest questions I hear. All of us wonder at some point if we should really expect to hear from God.

Maybe we think we've never heard God. Maybe we think we have. Maybe we want to. Maybe we don't. Maybe we think it's possible for some people, but not for us. Maybe we don't think it's possible at all (which means that we suspect people who claim to hear God are lying, either to themselves or to the rest of us). Either way, we wonder.

Does God speak?

If he does, could I hear him?

Today we're going to talk about how to hear God. We believe that *if* we learn to listen to the ways God communicates, *then* we will hear his voice. Yep, that's right. You can be one of the crazies. The people God talks to. But you're going to have to work at it a bit, because this kind of craziness doesn't come naturally.

The good news is that God does speak and you can learn to hear him. Jesus couldn't have said this any clearer:

> *The one who enters by the gate is the shepherd of the sheep. The gatekeeper opens the gate for him, and the sheep listen to his voice. He calls his own sheep by name and leads them out. When he has brought out all his own, he goes on ahead of them, and his sheep follow*

him because they know his voice. . . . I am the good shepherd; I know my sheep and my sheep know me. (John 10:2-4,14)

You can and will hear from God, but you must first learn how God communicates. If you learn to listen, then you will hear God speak.

For any relationship to develop, two people must learn how to listen to one another. On the simplest level, if two people don't speak the same language then meaningful communication will be difficult. *Come possiamo essere amici se non parla italiano?*

See what I mean?

So let's get to it. How does God "speak"?

Of course this includes knowing the kinds of things God might say. If a man called my wife from my phone and said, "God is fake and you're an idiot for believing in him," no matter how much this person's voice sounded like mine, she would know it wasn't me. That's just not something I would say. Same goes for God. There are some things he would never say. God would never tell you you're worthless. God would never tell you to commit murder or feed your greed or have sex with someone who isn't your husband or wife. As a general rule, just remember this: God will never say something to you that contradicts what he has revealed in the Bible. So as you study Scripture more and more, you will be better equipped to evaluate the content of a supposed "word from the Lord."

But you probably already knew that. What you need to discover is what David talks about in Psalm 19:1-4:

The heavens declare the glory of God;
   the skies proclaim the work of his hands.
Day after day they pour forth speech;
   night after night they reveal knowledge.
They have no speech, they use no words;
   no sound is heard from them.
Yet their voice goes out into all the earth,
   their words to the ends of the world.

When David looks up and sees a starry night, what does he see? More to our point, what does he hear? On the one hand, he hears nothing—*no speech, no words, no sound*. On the other hand, he hears quite a bit—*declaration, proclamation, words, a voice*.

Sometimes God speaks without saying a word. Think about it like this: When we communicate with one another, we are guiding each other's thoughts in a particular direction. When you're speaking with your mechanic, you are guiding his or her thoughts toward finding out what is wrong with your car. On a human level, we tend to do this with words. Words are tools we use to communicate. But as we said, sometimes we communicate without words—handshakes, hugs, the look, etc.

God in his greatness most often communicates without actually verbalizing words. Generally speaking, God "speaks" to us in one or more of the following ways:

(1) *Through Scripture.* The Bible is God's Word to us as well as its original hearers, and Jesus-followers from all ages agree that this is the primary way God communicates and reveals. People who regularly read the Bible hear God speaking more often than those who don't.

(2) *Through creation.* This is what David spoke about in Psalm 19. David looked at the vastness of creation—sun, moon, stars, mountains, oceans, etc.—and heard nonverbal whispers from God about God's power and care and attention.

(3) *Through people.* God often speaks to us through

one another—a pastor delivering a message, a parent reassuring us of love, a friend encouraging us to grow, an enemy criticizing our blind spots.

(4) *Through circumstances.* God is quite capable of communicating through the details of what is happening in your life right now. Not everything that happens is God speaking, which is why God often combines this form of communication with another.

If you want to hear God, these are the ways you must listen.

Day 3

If we seek God above all else
Then we will find him

Have you ever wondered if you might run out of air? Have you ever been so thirsty you literally wondered if your body might just shut down? Have you ever loved someone so much it hurt not to have her or him?

So far we've covered some important territory. We now know that to see God clearly we must fix our eyes on Jesus, for he is the place of God's clearest and fullest revelation.

We also learned that while God rarely "talks to us" like we talk to each other, he is always speaking. And we can hear him—we can recognize his voice—if only we learn how he communicates: today through a mountain or sunset, tomorrow through reading the Bible, here through a thought that pops into our head, there through a word or hug from a friend or our child.

With this knowledge we should have no problem developing a friendship with God based on truth and joyful interaction.

But most of us won't. Why? Because we don't want to.

We say we want to. And we say we want to because we think we want to. And in a sense, this is true. We do want to see and know God. We do want an engaging, interactive, enjoyable friendship with God. But we want lots of other things just as much, if not more. And as long as we want something other than God more than we want God, then we'll have to be content with something other than God.

God doesn't stick around where he's not wanted. God can't be truly known and enjoyed when he's not pursued first, when he's not desired *most*.

Moses knew this. He couldn't have been clearer than

in Deuteronomy 4.29: *But if from there you seek the LORD your God, you will find him if you seek him with all your heart and with all your soul.*

David knew this, as did Israel's other songwriters. We see it all over the book of Psalms. *One thing I ask from the LORD, this only do I seek: that I may dwell in the house of the LORD all the days of my life, to gaze on the beauty of the LORD and to seek him in his temple* (Ps 27.4). *As the deer pants for streams of water, so my soul pants for you, my God. My soul thirsts for God, for the living God. When can I go and meet with God?* (Ps 42.1-2). *You, God, are my God, earnestly I seek you; I thirst for you, my whole being longs for you, in a dry and parched land where there is no water* (Ps 63.1).

Paul knew this: *I consider everything a loss because of the surpassing worth of knowing Christ Jesus my Lord, for whose sake I have lost all things* (Phil 3.8).

God himself said through the prophet Jeremiah: *You will seek me and find me when you seek me with all your heart* (Jer 29.13).

One time Jesus walked up to a man who had been

invalid for almost forty years. Every day this guy got his friends to carry him to a healing pool in hopes that he might be cured. Do you know what Jesus asked him? *"Do you want to get well?"*

What do you want?

What kind of a question is that? You know what he wants. Of course he wants to get well. Right? Otherwise he wouldn't show up every day. Right? Or is it possible that sometimes we go through all the motions that would indicate we desire something when in fact we're just going through the motions.

Jesus' question is dumb unless you realize that desire—what we want—is everything. Desire is what determines whether we will genuinely open ourselves up to what God has for us. God will not force himself upon us. We must want him. We must want him more than anything.

One time a famous philosopher was approached by an extremely intelligent young man full of pride and ready to take on the world.[1]

---

[1] Story is recounted by M. Littleton in *Moody Monthly*, June 1989, p. 29

"O great wise sage, I come to thee seeking knowledge," he said with an air of airiness.

"Okay, follow me," the wise old man replied. He led the young man down into a river where he grabbed hold of the boy and held him under the water for about twenty seconds. He yanked the boy—now panting—out of the river and asked him a question.

"What do you want?"

"I want knowledge, O wise—"

Before he could finish, the philosopher dunked him again for the same amount of time.

"What do you want?"

"I want wisd—"

Again the boy's answer was violently interrupted by water. A third time he was raised up.

"I want air! Just give me some air!"

The philosopher smiled and said, "When you want knowledge as you now want air, you will have knowledge. When your want to be wise as desperately as

If we seek God above all else

you just wanted to breathe, you will find what you seek."

Whoever has ears to hear, let them hear.

What do you want?

Day 4

*If we love one another
Then God will dwell in our midst.*

Once upon a time there were two brothers who worked together on a family farm. The older brother had a wife and kids. The younger brother lived on his own. The two brothers always split their resources and profit fifty-fifty.

One night the older brother thought to himself, "My brother, whom I love very much, is vulnerable. He has no wife to care for him when he is sick, no children to look after him as he grows old. It is not right for me to take fifty percent of our profits. He should receive more. I must do what I can to help." So every night he would carry a bag of grain from his own bin and pour it into his younger brother's.

Around that same time the younger brother thought to himself, "My brother, for whom I have so much admiration and respect, has so much he is responsible for. He has a wife and children who adore him and who look to him to provide support. If something tragic were ever to happen, they would be in serious trouble. It is not right for me to take fifty percent of our profits. He should receive more. I must do what I can do help." So every night he too would carry a bag of grain from his own bin and pour it into his older brother's.

Both were puzzled for many months as to why their supply seemed not to dwindle.

One night the two brothers accidentally caught one another when their paths crossed unexpectedly. Once they realized what the other was doing, they dropped their bags of grain, their eyes filled with tears, and they embraced.

It is said that at that moment God looked down and chose that very spot to build his great Temple, for his presence belonged in the place where brothers came together in love.

Then God will dwell in our midst.

I don't know if the story is historically accurate, but it certainly tells the truth. Listen now to the words of the Apostle John in 1 John 4:12: *No one has ever seen God; but if we love one another, God lives in us and his love is made complete in us.*

The word John uses for "lives" means to *dwell* or *remain* in one place. God does not leave a place where brothers and sisters *love one another.*

When it comes to seeking God, we must remember that we never just seek God. To seek God is to love God's people.

I don't like people who don't like my wife and children. It's nothing personal. They may have great reasons for their lack of appreciation for my family's perfection. That's fine. But we will never be close friends.

If you're reading this book, I'm assuming you want to know God. You want to experience God. You want to love God. This is what we've been talking about all week. Knowing God starts with looking closely at Jesus, continues by learning to listen to the ways God speaks, and is always energized by desiring God above all else. All of this has been about your relationship with God, which will always be your most important relationship. God calls us to a relationship that is personal.

But he does not call us to a relationship that is private. You can't love God without loving people. You can't enjoy close friendship with God without learning to love God's family.

Did you know that God promises not to listen to my prayers if I'm not being kind to my wife? I'm not making this up. He couldn't have been clearer on this: *Husbands, in the same way be considerate as you live with your wives, and treat them with respect as the weaker partner and as heirs with you of the gracious gift of life, <u>so that nothing will hinder your prayers</u>* (1 Pet 3.7).

And what Peter teaches here doesn't just apply to marriage. Jesus himself taught that if you're at church worshiping God and remember that someone has an issue with you, you should stop worshiping immediately and resolve the conflict, and only then come back to finish worshiping.

God will neither speak nor listen when we don't actively love one another. The further we remove ourselves from the church—this community of brothers and sisters living together in the name of Jesus—the more distance we place between ourselves and God. If you want to see God and live in his presence, remember 1 John 4.12: *No one has ever seen God; but if we love one another, God lives in us and his love is made complete in us.*

Week 3

I Remain He Produces

Greed may be one of the most dangerous sins on earth, but like all sins it is actually the flip side of something good. The desire for *more* may kill you or even lead you to kill others (figuratively or literally), but the fact is you were created for *more* than you are probably currently experiencing.

In one sense that "more" is simply God. You've heard people say that we all have a God-shaped hole in our hearts. And if we try to fill that hole with other things—which we all do—we will be disappointed and, yes, brokenhearted. And you've heard that once we turn to God to be our God, we experience a peaceful rest that can't be found anywhere else. You may have even heard the famous prayer from Augustine: "Our heart is restless until it rests in you."[2]

God is the *more* you were created for. Doing life with God—a life of following Jesus—is the most satisfying, rewarding, truly restful way to spend your eighty-ish years (not to mention the rest of eternity).

But what if there is more to life with God than you first realized? The question is rhetorical, because both you and I know there is.

Maybe you're a brand new Jesus-follower. If so, that's awesome. Welcome to the family. I hope you're coming to know the hope and joy and peace that are only found in Christ. I imagine you are. I imagine you're learning new meanings to words like content and satisfied and rest.

Or maybe you're a longtime lover of God. You remember that initial sense of being overwhelmed by more life than you could have ever imagined. But eventually it wore off. Or at least it felt like it wore off.

---

[2] St. Augustine, *Confessions* (Trans. Henry Chadwick. Oxford University Press, 2009), p. 3.

Actually it didn't wear off at all. You just grew.

By "grew" in this case, I mean you caught up to this new level of being alive. You got used to knowing God. This isn't bad, it means you are becoming the person you were meant to be.

But it is very important that you don't misunderstand what is happening (or happened; or, if you are a newbie, will happen). You are not any further from God than you were. But you are experiencing the very natural and positive desire for more. Not for more *than* God, mind you, but for more *of* God.

Or maybe, more specifically, more of the life you know God wants from and for you. You are not the person you were before you met Jesus, but your "growth curve" has flattened out. You stagnated a bit. You're not as impatient as before, but you still wouldn't describe yourself as thoroughly patient. Speaking gentle and kind words no longer feels like ripping off your fingernails with a pair of pliers, but it still doesn't come naturally to you. You no longer fear the same things—challenges, relationships, difficult conversations—but you'd love to have more courage, more faith that God can do anything through you.

You want to grow. You want to be better. You want to produce more fruit.

And you can. This week we're going to talk about how. But we have to start with a very simple, but powerful, teaching of Jesus from John 15:1-8.

> *I am the true vine, and my Father is the gardener. He cuts off every branch in me that bears no fruit, while every branch that does bear fruit he prunes so that it will be even more fruitful. You are already clean because of the word I have spoken to you. Remain in me, as I also remain in you. No branch can bear fruit by itself; it must remain in the vine. Neither can you bear fruit unless you remain in me.*
>
> *I am the vine; you are the branches. If you remain in me and I in you, you will bear much fruit; apart from me you can do nothing. If you do not remain in me, you are like a branch that is thrown away and withers; such branches are picked up, thrown into the fire and burned. If you remain*

in me and my words remain in you, ask whatever you wish, and it will be done for you. This is to my Father's glory, that you bear much fruit, showing yourselves to be my disciples.

Here Jesus talks about the core principle of growing, of becoming more productive in your spiritual life. You must stay connected to Jesus. Practically speaking, how can you do that? Keep reading and find out.

———————————

For a deeper look at this content and to actually see/hear this message brought 'to life' in front of the congregation at Real Life Church, please go to www.reallifechurch.org/ifthen/week3.

Day 1

*If we put sin to death
Then God's life will flow through us.*

Jesus came to give us new life, but that life will only flourish if we let it.

Jesus didn't come from heaven to earth to help you clean up your act a bit. He didn't bid farewell to the joy of celestial bliss so that you and I could experience a little self-improvement. He came because you and I are currently living in a state of death. This death is obviously not total—we're still here, after all. We are not dead dead, even if we haven't received Jesus as Savior and Lord. But we are dead in the sense that we're cut off from the life of God.

Think about it like this. As human beings, you could

say that we are made up of body, soul, and spirit. Our body is the physical location of who we are, and we use our bodies to interact with the world around us. Our soul is the immaterial dimension—the part that can't be seen or measured or mapped by a telescope. Our thoughts, feelings, fears, and desires are all part of our soul.

We are alive when our body and soul are functioning normally. Everyone you've interacted with today has a functioning body and soul. Some bodies and souls are healthier than others, but even the unhealthy ones work to some extent. When they stop working, we die.

Then there's our spirit. We could use the word "spirit" in many different ways, but I'm using it to refer to the part of us that connects to God. Without Jesus, that part of us is dead. That's what Paul meant when he wrote that we are "dead in [our] transgressions and sins" (Eph 2:1). Without Jesus, we are not functioning as designed because we are disconnected from God.

We're like a sailboat on a windless morning or a computer that isn't plugged in. The source of our life and

Then God's life will flow through us.

power has been cut off. Jesus came to turn it back on, to plug us in, to put the wind back in our sails. (Okay, that was cheesy. But you get the point.)

Someone once said that Jesus didn't come to make bad people good. He came to bring dead people back to life.

That's good news.

But the life that Jesus brings—the rehabilitation of our spirits—won't maintain itself. Biological life and spiritual life often work the same way. Our biological life is not something we made for ourselves, but we can certainly take it away—whether all at once in suicide or slowly over time with bad health habits. In the same way, we can't generate the spiritual life that Jesus breathes into us, but we can stop its flow.

How? I don't mean to over-simplify matters, but the way we clog our spiritual arteries is pretty simple: we sin. In any number of ways, we look at what we know God wants for us and say, "No thanks."

It's an obviously dumb decision when we put it this directly, but it's nonetheless a decision we make daily.

Everyone eats the apple.

Dumb. And deadly. Suicidal isn't too strong a word, in fact. Look at what Paul says in Romans 8:13: *If you live according to the flesh, you will die; but if by the Spirit you put to death the misdeeds of the body, you will live.*

That's Paul's fancy way of saying that when you choose your sin over God's will, you cut yourself off from God's life. God's Spirit carries God's life to your Spirit, but your sin tells God's Spirit to go away.

Sin has the power to kill you. Which is why Paul tells you to *put sin to death* before it gets the chance. Of all the things to do with sin, *put to death* doesn't always appear at the top of our list.

We typically prefer to *justify* our sins. *Cut me some slack, I'm doing the best I can. You should've seen how badly I used to sin.* The very religious among us prefer a more sophisticated form of justifying sin: We *debate* sin. Whose sin is worse? Yours? Mine? Theirs?

I once heard someone say that the worst sin is the one you're about to commit. I think Paul would agree.

Then God's life will flow through us.

Whatever sin you're staring in the face right now—envy, gossip, greed, unbridled anger, lust—is the one you need to take seriously. And by take seriously, we mean *put it to death*. And by put it to death, we mean don't do it!

Day 2

If we meditate on God's words
Then we will be stable and productive.

I recently heard about a lady whose church shut down their women's ministry. She went to the pastor and complained that she needed to study the Bible with other women. He told her not to let this decision stop her and to go find some women to study with out in the world. Long story short, she wound up starting a Bible study with some inmates in a nearby women's prison. The study became a hit, blessing both this woman and the ladies she taught. Matter of fact, one of the ladies came up for early parole, but—I'm not making this up—she asked if she could stay in prison an extra two weeks until their study was over.

I rarely meet a Jesus-follower who thinks they read the Bible enough. Everyone seems to agree that we need to read more than we do. Yet most of us never make noticeable changes to our Bible reading routine (or lack thereof). Why?

Why don't *you* read the Bible more?

At the end of the day, the reason is simple: We don't think we need to. I know you would never say that. We prefer more palatable reasons such as "I'm not a big reader" or "I don't understand what I'm reading" or "I don't know where to start." But truth be told, those are smokescreens. They're excuses. I'm not saying they're not true, but they're not the core reason we don't read the Bible more. The core reason, once again, is simple: we don't think we need to.

Imagine if your child became deathly ill and you had the power to cure them. But the cure to this particular illness could only be discovered by reading *War and Peace*. Reading *War and Peace* just might kill you, but there's no question about whether you would do it. Why? Because you'd have to. Because something is at stake that you're not willing to lose.

Then we will be stable and productive.

We don't believe enough is at stake when it comes to reading Scripture. Otherwise we'd find a way to do it. Even those of us who don't read would find a way to do it. But we don't find a way to do it, because we think we can get what we need without it.

What if we're wrong?

The inmate stayed in prison so she could finish a Bible study. Why? What would motivate such seemingly ridiculous behavior? The only answer is that whatever the Bible was giving her was absolutely necessary, and therefore more important than getting out of jail.

What if the only path to a truly abundant life cuts right through the rarely easy, sometimes exciting, often confusing, occasionally boring process of reading and meditating on Scripture?

These ladies discovered the truth of Psalm 1:1-3:
> *Blessed is the one*
> > *who does not walk in step with the wicked*
> *or stand in the way that sinners take*
> > *or sit in the company of mockers,*
> *but whose delight is in the law of the Lord,*
> > *and who meditates on his law day and night.*

That person is like a tree planted by streams of water,

which yields its fruit in season
and whose leaf does not wither—

whatever they do prospers.

You could also look at Joshua 1:8, Psalm 119:105, or 2 Timothy 3:16. They all make the same claim: you can't live a full life without paying attention to Scripture. Meditating on Scripture means slowly dwelling on the words, letting them sink in, turning them over and over in your mind. Do this and, like a firmly rooted, well-watered tree, you will *yield fruit in season.*

You will find yourself capable of doing the right thing in every situation.

Reading the Bible gives God a great opportunity to speak to you. Reading the Bible forces you to examine your assumptions about who God is. Reading the Bible teaches you whether what you're doing is right or wrong. Reading the Bible equips you to help other people find answers to their spiritual questions. In short, reading the Bible uniquely trains you to live well.

So where do we go from here? I could tell stories or

Then we will be stable and productive.

provide statistics that support my case, but that probably won't work. You've heard it all before. In the end, all I can do is dare you to give it a shot. Get a Bible, make a plan, and stick to it. Start reading and studying and memorizing and meditating on Scripture and see for yourself.

Day 3

If we ask God for wisdom
Then God will give it to us.

Let's start with a few games today. First, let's imagine you found yourself in a real-life movie with a genie, a bottle, and a decision about what to wish for. We'll say your genie is generous and offers you four wishes—anything you want (except, as everyone knows, no wishing for someone's death and no wishing for more wishes). What would you wish for?

If you paid attention to the title of today's chapter, you know where I'm going with this: Did you wish for wisdom? If so, why? If not, why not?

Now let's play a little word association game today.

When you hear the word "wisdom," what comes to mind?

Don't rush through this. Really give it some time. What is wisdom? What is it for? Who has it? Do you have it? How would you know? How would it help if you did?

Do you think about a definition for wisdom, or maybe a person you consider wise? Do you imagine situations in which wisdom might be needed? Do you remember wise advice from a mentor or grandparent?

Now we can be done with the games, but I do have a few more questions for you: Do you think wisdom is desirable? Or better yet, *how* desirable is it? How badly do you want wisdom? Why?

To say nothing else, the Bible teaches that wisdom is something we should want. If you've spent much time with the Bible or in church, you probably know the story of Solomon, one of Israel's great kings. God once promised Solomon that he would offer him anything he asked. If we didn't know the story, we'd probably say that Solomon would ask for wealth, or maybe a long and successful reign as king, or the

Then God will give it to us.

death of a rival. But Solomon doesn't ask for any of these things. He asks for wisdom.

Solomon believed nothing was more valuable—and therefore nothing was more desirable—than wisdom. God didn't disappoint, and according to Solomon's teachings in the book of Proverbs, he never regretted asking for wisdom:

> *Blessed are those who find wisdom,*
> > *those who gain understanding,*
> *for she is more profitable than silver*
> > *and yields better returns than gold.*
> *She is more precious than rubies;*
> > *nothing you desire can compare with her.*
>
> (Prov 3:13-15)

Once again, the Bible teaches that wisdom is something we should want. Something we should ask for. Why? Well, it's simple really. Because we have to live. We have to make decisions and judgment calls. We have to choose to do one thing rather than countless others. And wisdom is the skill of knowing what to do. Wisdom is the ability to discern what is best in any given situation.

Do you ever wonder what to do?

I do. That's why I should want wisdom. You, too. That's why we should ask for wisdom.

You might be interested to know that this is always a prayer that God answers—as long as we pray it sincerely. James (the brother of Jesus) writes: *If any of you lacks wisdom, you should ask God, who gives generously to all without finding fault, and it will be given to you* (Jas 1.5).

Pretty simple, right? Two additional points, one from what the text says and another from what the text doesn't say.

First, we can't read James 1:5 apart from James 1:6-8: *But when you ask, you must believe and not doubt, because the one who doubts is like a wave of the sea, blown and tossed by the wind. That person should not expect to receive anything from the Lord. Such a person is double-minded and unstable in all they do.*

You've got to believe that God will give you wisdom. You can't ask God for wisdom one minute and then lean on the world's wisdom the next. If you really want wisdom, you've got to trust 100 percent that God's voice is the one you'll listen to. Otherwise it makes

Then God will give it to us.

no sense for God to show you the way since the way of God isn't always easy and you might think God is crazy when he gives you what you're asking for.

Second, notice the word you don't find anywhere in this promise: *immediately*. For much of my life I didn't believe this verse, primarily because of experience. I would find myself in a situation where I needed wisdom, so I would ask for it. Then nothing would happen. I figured either James was wrong or I doubted, but either way it didn't seem to be working.

Then I started to see a pattern. God was giving me wisdom, just not right away. Over time God wove together various threads in my life to provide the wisdom I needed. Then I realized that there's no time stamp on God's promise through James. God will always give wisdom when we ask, even if it sometimes takes a while.

So . . . if any of you lacks wisdom, you should ask God, who gives generously to all without finding fault, and it will be given to you.

Day 4

If we pay attention
to God's presence and power
Then God will provide peace.

Wherever you are, God is.

In just a minute, I want you to close this book and look around. (Hold on a second, not yet!) Here in a bit, I want you to notice as many details as you can see. If you're outside, look up at the sky. Is it gray? Blue? Cloudy? Clear? If you're inside, look around the room. What do you see on the walls, the floor, the counter top? What are you sitting on? What kind of light are you reading with? I want you to look around and take in as much as possible. Do you see people? Movement? Buildings? Benches? Flowers? Trees?

Okay, I think you get the point. Go for it.

Now I want you to list below as many details as you can remember:

_____

_____

_____

_____

_____

_____

_____

_____

Your eyes probably took in quite a bit, even more than you remembered or wrote down. And here's my point in all this: Whatever is on your list is on God's list, too. If we asked God to do the same exercise right now, he would write down every detail you mentioned as well as those you saw but forgot to write down (not to mention the kajillion things you missed). Why? Because wherever you are, God is.

Because. God. Is. Always. With. You. Everywhere you go. In everything you do. In front of everyone you see. God is there. Or here, as it were.

Don't believe me? Don't just take my word for it.

> *Where can I go from your Spirit? Where can I flee from your presence? If I go up to the heavens, you are there; if I make my bed in the depths, you are there. If I rise on the wings of the dawn, if I settle on the far side of the sea, even there your hand will guide me, your right hand will hold me fast. (Ps 139:7-10)*

You could also read Deuteronomy 31:6, Proverbs 15:3, Acts 17:26-27, or Matthew 28:20. They all make the same point: God is with you.

Seriously think about this for a minute. I'm convinced that no standard "Christian belief" is more routinely ignored than this one. We believe that God is everywhere, which means we believe that God is here. We live our entire lives in the presence of the holy, righteous, massively powerful, unbelievably wise, overwhelmingly loving creator of the universe. Yet we go about our daily routines hardly thinking about it! We somehow manage to ignore the fact that God is with us—that he is always wherever we are.

Imagine just how much God sees when he looks around. He knows exactly how many hairs are on the head of every person. He can tell you the precise length, width, and weight of every blade of grass beneath you. Every tree exhibits his creativity and every flower manifests his joy. He invented the color of the sky above your head and the texture of the dirt under your feet. He knows and he sees everything.

Think about all that knowledge and wisdom. And all that power! God is where you are, and he is entirely sovereign over every detail of everything. He is working all things together not only for your good, but for the good of all.

God's presence and power are the key to your peace.

Listen to what Paul wrote in Philippians 4:5-7:

Then God will provide peace.

The Lord is near. Do not be anxious about anything, but in every situation, by prayer and petition, with thanksgiving, present your requests to God. And the peace of God, which transcends all understanding, will guard your hearts and your minds in Christ Jesus.

He is talking about prayer, of course. But the key to prayer is not prayer. The key to prayer is God. And because of who God is, we can know peace when everything in our world trends toward chaos and fear.

Let's imagine this was our only Bible verse on the topic of prayer. What would we know about prayer if this were all we had?

Prayer is rooted in the nearness of God. We're not talking to a God far away, but to a God who is wherever we are.

Prayer is the appropriate response to every situation. No occasion is too big or too small to become an opportunity to pray.

Prayer involves us asking God for things. This is what "petition" means. Prayer is more than asking God for stuff, but it is not less.

If we pay attention to God's presence and power

Prayer should be characterized by a spirit of thanksgiving. Even as we ask for something new, we must never forget what God has already given.

When we pray, God will provide peace. As we learned yesterday about asking for wisdom, this may not come immediately or automatically. But it will come.

I'd say that's a pretty good foundation to build on! With that in mind, make a list below of everything in your life (past, present, or future) that could produce anxiety.

_____

_____

_____

_____

_____

_____

_____

_____

_____

Then God will provide peace.

Remember that God is already present in every one of those situations. Then ask God for whatever you think you need, and rest in knowing that God will do whatever is best.

Week 4

I Obey
He Blesses

You ever have that "I never noticed that before" moment? It may be with a restaurant in a strip mall near your house, it may be a scratch on the side of your car, or it may be the grey hairs creeping into your beard. We've all had that experience with common things in our life that we get used to overlooking. Some of us have even had that with the Bible. I know that happens to me often. I read something and think, "Has that always been there?" or "How did I overlook that?" A few years ago, when I was doing my daily reading in the Bible, I came across such a thing that greatly impacted my life.

I guess I thought I'd seen it all in the Bible. After all, I grew up in the church. My parents saw to it that I was there three times a week. And when you are there that often, you cover a lot of Bible. From there I went to a Christian college where the Bible was my textbook. After graduation I became a Pastor where the Bible was my employee handbook. All these years and hours of reading the Bible, and one day I noticed something I'd never noticed before. It wasn't a name I'd overlooked, or a geography clarification I'd missed, it was something so huge and life altering it changed everything for me. And I pray it will do the same for you.

The passage comes at the end of what is referred to as Jesus' Sermon on the Mount. Matthew records this message in his account of Jesus life. It's found in the book of Matthew, chapters five to seven. Jesus is teaching this amazing message to the disciples and all the onlookers. He encourages them, he challenges them, he clarifies his relationship to the law they'd been taught to keep all their lives, and he even gives some specific if/then statements for everyone. There are some heavy topics in this message: marriage, divorce, revenge, anger, commitments, justice, and worrying just to name a few. But it's the conclusion of the message that shook me up.

Jesus tells the story of two men who go out to build a house.

> *Therefore everyone who hears these words of mine and puts them into practice is like a wise man who built his house on the rock. The rain came down, the streams rose, and the winds blew and beat against that house; yet it did not fall, because it had its foundation on the rock. But everyone who hears these words of mine and does not put them into practice is like a foolish man who built his house on sand. The rain came down, the streams rose, and the winds blew and beat against that house, and it fell with a great crash. (Matt 7:24-27)*

I guess I'd heard so many sermons imploring me to not build my house on the sand that I missed the "how to". In this wrap up to the greatest message ever preached, Jesus states how to not only avoid the sand, but how to build your life on the rock.

He says:

> *"Everyone who hears these words of mine and puts them into practice."*

Here's the way I used to read that:

> *"Everyone who hears these words of mine."*

And that was it. So I made it my mission to just hear more. I took classes, I joined groups, learned all the methods of Biblical study. My whole life was about consuming more and more knowledge. But what I had missed, and what I finally noticed, was the second half of that verse:

> *"AND puts them into practice."*

It wasn't enough to *learn*; I had to *use* what I'd learned. It wasn't enough to *study*; I had to put it into *action*. I once heard Pastor Randy Frazee tell a story of inviting the great theologian J.I. Packer to his church to observe their discipleship process. After spending some time with their church, Packer said: "You know what your problem is? You all study the Bible too much." Frazee was a bit stunned. Packer concluded "Your people are in five Bible studies a week, but have no dirt under their nails from working with the poor."[3]

That was the moment I decided: I don't want to be just a learner of the word of God, I want to be a practitioner of it. Our participation with God is not based on how much we know, but rather on how much we apply what we know.

This week of our study will be about the things Jesus tells us in this great sermon that we are to not just know, but we are to do. It's not enough to hear; we must also do. And Jesus says when we do both, we'll build such a life that when the storms of life come, our house will not fall.

For a deeper look at this content and to actually see/hear this message brought 'to life' in front of the congregation at Real Life Church, please go to www.reallifechurch.org/ifthen/week4.

---

[3] Frazee details his church's subsequent transformation in *The Connecting Church* (Grand Rapids: Zondervan, 2001).

Day 1

If we let our light shine
Then others will glorify God

Ever watch a movie that is so good you want everyone you know and love to see it as soon as possible? Or maybe it's a great restaurant you recently visited. It was so good, you take a friend to it the very next day. We all want others to share in amazing experiences we've had and the excitement we've found—even when It's our relationship with God.

Many of us have had that experience where we start going to church, we have a great experience, we begin our faith journey, we grow in our relationship with Jesus, and then we think of all the people in our lives that we wish could find what we've now found. But often we hesitate saying anything about it. We justify it by saying things like, "Oh, they wouldn't understand," or "It's a personal thing."

One of the dangers in only hearing the word of God and not practicing it is that you never share it. I reached a point in my life where I realized that not only was I not sharing the word of God with anyone who was far from God, I didn't even *know* anyone who was far from God. Everyone in my world was a Christ follower. So when I'd read that Jesus said to be a fisher of men, I'd think, *Yes, someone should do that.* But I didn't know anyone who needed to be "caught."

Partnering with God and his plan for my life means that I become part of his renovation project of this world. That plan is for people who are far from him to come near—and God enlists us to help. So, why is it that we who find and come to know God retreat further away from the people God still misses?

For some, it's because we are afraid of returning to our old lives. We fear if we associate with non-Christians, it might tempt us to slip back into a previous lifestyle.

For others, we are intimidated or nervous about our

faith and fear being asked questions we can't answer.

For many of us, we think people who knew our old life might see us as hypocrites.

But the great thing about participating with God in his plan to save the world is that it has nothing to do with our perfection or our intellect. Nor does it have anything to do with a need to get a bullhorn and a sandwich board and stand on the corner.

Take a look at what Jesus says in his Sermon on the Mount:

> *In the same way, let your light shine before others, that they may see your good deeds and glorify your Father in heaven. (Matt 5:16)*

IF we let our light shine . . . THEN people direct their attention to God.

The question is: What does it mean to let our light shine before men?

Paul tells us in Romans 2:4 something interesting about the nature of God and his light that shines. He says that it is the "kindness" of God that leads us to repentance. In other words, it is not the judgment of God, the intellect of God, the logic of God, or the condemnation of God that compels us to follow him, but rather his kindness.

Jesus certainly modeled this. We already saw how he extended kindness to Matthew, extended grace to a woman caught in adultery, and extended mercy to Zacchaeus, and on and on. What I've learned is you cannot *share* the truth of Jesus without *doing* it in the spirit of Jesus.

So, having been convicted of this in my own life, I decided to just start with extending kindness to people in my neighborhood and see where God took it. We had people over for dinner, I mowed neighbors' lawns, my wife baked cookies, our kids invited other kids over, we went on vacations with them, we went to concerts, we even went and watched friends sing at a karaoke bar. And what started as a way to hopefully share Christ quickly became a joy to be in community with dear friends, and eventually they started to take steps on their own spiritual journey.

Since we got serious about letting our light shine

we've had the privilege to see our neighbors come to church, come to faith, get baptized, lead in ministries, join Bible studies, and eventually start bringing their own friends to church as well. Since we've been partnering with God in practicing the words of Jesus, we've seen our friends far from God grow to glorify God with their lives.

For years I'd hoped to see people experience what I had through Jesus, and by participating with God in their lives I finally had that pleasure.

Day 2

If we honor him
Then he'll reward us

What I love about our statement today is that it reminds us that God wants to reward us. He wants to bless us with his friendship, his voice, his provision, his leadership, and even his comfort. He wants to reward us with the treasures of grace and mercy. He wants to overwhelm us with beauty and joy, and he wants to direct us into his purpose and plan for our lives, which will bring ultimate satisfaction. But he only wants to do this if we are ready for it.

We're talking about doing more than just being a spectator to the blessings and activity of God, we're talking about participating in it. And the participation today has more to do with the "why" we do it than the "how."

Look what Jesus says in Matthew 6:

> Be careful not to practice your righteousness in front of others to be seen by them. If you do, you will have no reward from your Father in heaven.
>
> So when you give to the needy, do not announce it with trumpets, as the hypocrites do in the synagogues and on the streets, to be honored by others. Truly I tell you, they have received their reward in full. But when you give to the needy, do not let your left hand know what your right hand is doing, so that your giving may be in secret. Then your Father, who sees what is done in secret, will reward you.
>
> And when you pray, do not be like the hypocrites, for they love to pray standing in the synagogues and on the street corners to be seen by others. Truly I tell you, they have received their reward in full. But when you pray, go into your room, close the door and pray to your Father,

who is unseen. Then your Father, who sees what is done in secret, will reward you. And when you pray, do not keep on babbling like pagans, for they think they will be heard because of their many words. Do not be like them, for your Father knows what you need before you ask him. (Matt 6:1-8)

Where we get confused with this passage is when we think,

I guess Jesus is against public prayer. None of us should pray in public, pray before a meal, pray in church. It's a personal thing, so keep it to yourself.

I guess Jesus is against repetitive prayers. We shouldn't pray very long, we shouldn't repeat anything. Say it once, silently, and move on.

I guess Jesus is against giving my offering in church. I don't want anyone to know I'm giving so I should only give online, never make a pledge to a church building campaign, and never tell stories about my giving to anyone.

The truth is Jesus isn't against public prayer, he's not against repetition, he's not against sharing your offering or even your offering story in church. He's asking this question: When you do all that, who's your primary audience?

In my profession I have a chance to speak before people every weekend. And in doing that, I have a chance to tell stories about my life, my family, and my friends. Occasionally there is an opportunity to share how much someone means to me or how grateful I am for someone in my life. How do you think my wife would feel if the only time I expressed how I felt about her was from stage? For instance, what if on Mother's Day I told several stories about why I think she's an amazing mom, but when I came home I said nothing. Or what if on the Sunday near Valentine's Day I told stories of my undying love and affection for my wife, but I didn't take her to dinner, buy her flowers or even a card? She would begin to suspect that my feelings about her were only expressed when they made ME look good.

Here's what Jesus is driving at: *make me your main audience, and I'll bring you far greater rewards than other people's approval ever could.*

A few suggestions:

Set a time and place: When will you meet with your Heavenly Father? Where can you be free from distractions?

Bring a notepad: Use it for writing down things that God may bring to mind, but also use it to write down the list of things to do that will come to mind. Once you jot them down, then you can get back to talking to God.

Be real: Jesus is steering us away from flowery words and lengthy soliloquies. Just shoot straight with God. Not only can he handle it, he encourages it.

I've noticed in my own life, that when I make private time with God a priority, it impacts my public life. My need for approval, my need for recognition, my need to be right all dissipates. In other words, the more I make God my primary audience, the less I need the approval of a larger audience. And not only that, God's rewards begin to stack up—his friendship, his leadership, his gentle words and directional wisdom.

If I choose to honor him / he rewards me—and he will you too.

Day 3

If we practice purity
Then we'll find intimacy

All of us want to have a great marriage.

If you are single, you hope to one day get married and have such a great marriage that Disney will make a movie about it.

If you are married, you hope your marriage does far more than just survive; you want it to succeed. You want the passion, romance, excitement, chemistry—all the things that made you fall in love with your spouse and get married in the first place.

And all of us want intimacy. It's not a word that guys are likely to say, but we know what it means. In sports, we call this camaraderie. That feeling of "we are in this thing together!" or "I've got your back!" It's feeling that there is someone in your life that you fully know—and you are fully known by them.

This was God's intent as well. When Adam and Eve were created, they were made for so much more than just reproduction, but to fill the void of being alone that God said was "not good."

> *The LORD God said, "It is not good for the man to be alone. I will make a helper suitable for him." (Gen 2:18)*

Look at how the Bible describes their connection:

> *So the LORD God caused the man to fall into a deep sleep; and while he was sleeping, he took one of the man's ribs and closed up the place with flesh. Then the LORD God made a woman from the rib he had taken out of the man, and he brought her to the man. The man said,*
>
> *"This is now bone of my bones and flesh of my flesh; she shall be called 'woman,' for she was taken out of man."*

That is why a man leaves his father and mother and is united to his wife, and they become one flesh. Adam and his wife were both naked, and they felt no shame. (Gen 2:21-25)

Camaraderie and companionship are at the heart of this first marriage. They are known and fully known. In fact, they feel no shame with each other.

But sin has a way of changing that. Once sin enters the world, it changes the relationship between not just man and God, but even between Adam and Eve. Suddenly, they feel shame; they discover pain, emptiness, loneliness, and the beginning of family conflict. It was the first time that a man says, "It's all her fault!" And ever since, we've been learning the bitter lesson of how our sin impacts our relational connection with each other. In short, our impurity ruins our intimacy.

Thousands of years later, we still see how our impurity impacts our intimacy. We see this in the broad strokes of words like lying, cheating, abuse, abandonment, and adultery. But it begins to manifest itself in the seemingly small acts of viewing pornography, Internet relationships, and flirtation with coworkers and neighbors. We tend to think these behaviors are fine because they aren't technically cheating, but Jesus reminds us that purity is bigger than just NOT having an affair.

This is what Jesus is driving at when he says in Matthew 5:27-30:

> You have heard that it was said, "You shall not commit adultery." But I tell you that anyone who looks at a woman lustfully has already committed adultery with her in his heart. If your right eye causes you to stumble, gouge it out and throw it away. It is better for you to lose one part of your body than for your whole body to be thrown into hell. And if your right hand causes you to stumble, cut it off and throw it away. It is better for you to lose one part of your body than for your whole body to go into hell.

Jesus is saying this: It's not about just avoiding physical unfaithfulness. Rather, be so committed to purity that you avoid mental unfaithfulness as well.

For years, Andy Stanley has been saying it this way: "Purity paves the way to intimacy."[4] We can't spend all

---
4 Andy Stanley, *The Seven Checkpoints For Student Leaders* (NY: Howard Books, 2011), p. 82.

Then we'll find intimacy

of our time praying for a great marriage and expecting our spouse to be our soul companion when we are unwilling to participate in purity. We all want intimacy, but we often avoid practicing the purity it will take to provide it.

What might you need to remove? A Facebook friend, a television channel, a way you travel to work? What might you need to add? Internet blocks, a friend that holds you accountable, memorizing this verse to remember when you are tempted?

Jesus would say the quickest way to develop intimacy, and all the joy that comes with it, is to do your part and practice purity. Become a person who is not just pure by avoiding adultery, but one who maintains purity even in your mind.

Day 4

If we seek him first
Then we'll be free from worry

So much of everything we've talked about in this book comes down to this if/then statement. It comes right at the crux of Jesus' message in the Sermon on the Mount and is the one that is often the easiest to hear and even repeat, but the hardest to do.

> *But seek first his kingdom and his righteousness, and all these things will be given to you as well. (Matt 6:33)*

If you put God and his (capital K) Kingdom first, *then* he'll take care of your (little k) kingdom.

The reason that we resist this is because we are not so sure that God has our best interest in mind. So, we need to worry and stress about our kingdom every day and show mild concern about his kingdom occasionally at church. This then leads us to live out our days worried, stressed, frustrated, lacking joy, and hoping and sometimes praying that things work out for us. It's no coincidence that Jesus precedes this statement with a warning against worry.

See, Jesus knows what we often overlook: Worry is not an issue of emotion, but a problem of devotion. We only worry about things we are devoted to.

For instance, I'm a Lakers fan. I don't worry about what the Washington Wizards do. I'm not checking their scores or stressing about their trades. I also worry about my kids. I worry about their grades, but I don't worry about your kids' grades. I want nothing but the best for your kids, but I'm not calling you at 9:00 p.m. asking if they got their homework done. Because I'm not devoted to your kids. And you're not devoted to my kids, either. We only worry about what we're devoted to. So, Jesus' solution for this and all of our worries and stresses in life is this: *change your devotion.*

Now I realize this is easier said than done. In fact, let me be perfectly honest with you: My name is Rusty and I'm a worrier. Part of it is just my personality. I'm a little high strung, a little OCD, I had an ulcer in the second grade. But part of it, I justify—I'm not worried, I'm just concerned. I'm just looking for worst-case scenarios. I don't like surprises. But here's where I get stuck: I know God *can*, but I don't know if He *will*. So I obsess over things and try to take control of things I can't control!

God says, "Trust me."

"Yes, but what if you don't fix it the way I'd fix it?"

God says, "Then I guess you still have to trust me."

I've learned a lot over my years about this issue and here's what I've discovered: If I only worry about what I'm devoted to, what if I just changed my devotion? That's what Jesus says to do.

> *Seek the Kingdom of God above all else, and live righteously, and he will give you everything you need (Matt 6:33 NLT)*

When I seek first *God's* kingdom, I worry a lot less.

But when I seek first my kingdom, I worry a lot more. Ninety-nine percent of my worry is wrapped around controlling *my* kingdom—my stuff, my comfort, my success, my approval, my happiness. But when I change my devotion to *his* kingdom, I worry less and he takes care of *my* kingdom. This doesn't mean you won't be concerned, or you won't get nervous, but you'll know whom you are with because you've become devoted to HIS Kingdom, rather than yours.

Once you become devoted to his kingdom, it does more than reduce your worry—it makes decision-making easier. Suddenly you are not weighing decisions based on how it will affect you, but just doing what pleases the Lord.

I had the chance to interview former NBA star A.C. Green. During his playing career he became known for more than just his talent on the court, but his reputation off the court. Though A.C. was a single guy living the life of an NBA star, he had made a decision to remain a virgin until marriage. He took a lot of heat from his teammates and the press even made some jokes at his expense. When I asked him about his decision to take a stand for abstinence, he said,

"It really wasn't about taking a stand for abstinence. It was about seeking first the kingdom of God. And God said to wait, so I waited. It was that simple."

I guess it can be that simple. As my friend Mike Breaux likes to say, "Following Jesus isn't easy, but it's not complicated." And when you decide to seek God first, it makes the rest of it a lot simpler. And I don't worry about things that are simple.

Week 5

I Serve
He Multiplies

You ever wonder what one person could possibly do to help God's mission move forward? You might be surprised to find that the answer isn't all that complicated.

Love is probably the most obvious one word answer. We move God's mission forward by actively loving others in all sorts of ways.

Jesus said that it was specifically our love that would identify us before a watching world. How would the world know who we are? By our love (see John 13:34-35). In other words, Jesus will work through our acts of love to draw people to himself. That's called multiplication—we do something small, God turns it into something big.

Another example from the Gospel of John is unity. Jesus prayed specifically that we would get along well with other followers of Jesus—even those with whom we might disagree on a few points. And not only did he pray for us to maintain unity, he actually said that it was because of our unity that people would believe that Jesus really was the heaven-sent Messiah (see John 17). Once again that's called multiplication: all we have to do is get along and God will work through that to draw people in.

But *love* is pretty vague. What if we got more specific? What one-word answer could we give that puts a finer point on it?

I can't think of a better candidate than *serve*. Just before Jesus said the words we referenced above about people knowing who we are because of our love, he helped define precisely what he meant.

Back in the first part of John 13, Jesus and his disciples walk into a room for a meal. Normally one of the household slaves would go around the room with a basin and towel and wash everyone's feet—an important task in a dusty pre-sneaker world. But for some reason the slave hadn't done his or her duty. Everyone would have known this, yet none of Jesus' followers did anything about it. But Jesus did. He grabbed the basin and the towel, and proceeded around the room washing the feet of everyone present.

He then said in no uncertain terms that as the Master has done, so the disciples must imitate. As followers of Jesus, you and I are called to serve.

And when we serve, God multiplies our small efforts into more than we could ever imagine.

This week we're going to look at a few of the ways we are called to serve. We'll explore questions like: What should we do and how should we do it? How do all our efforts work together as a team? How do we know that our efforts are worth it, especially when our new servant mindset only seems to make life harder?

This may be the part of the book where you are tempted to stop. You figure you've read more of this book than any other since your school days, so you're probably good. Don't let the enemy tempt you in this

I Serve

way. If we stop before talking about serving, we're missing out on so many of the great promises God has offered. But if we do serve . . . well, you'll just have to keep reading to find out.

For a deeper look at this content and to actually see/hear this message brought 'to life' in front of the congregation at Real Life Church, please go to www.reallifechurch.org/ifthen/week5.

Day 1

If we invest our finances in the mission
Then our joy will overflow

I once heard a money story about Erwin McManus, lead pastor of Mosaic Church in Los Angeles. A couple visited his church and met with him afterwards to ask a few questions. One question was somewhat vague: "Is this a *grace church* or a *law church*?" When McManus asked for clarification, they explained that their previous church was a *law church* because they demanded that every member tithe (which means to give ten percent of their earnings to the church to be used for ministry).

McManus's response was brilliant: "Oh, we're a *grace*

church—we expect way more than that!"[5]

Money is such a sensitive subject, especially when it comes to church. Let me put it like this: Let's say your church is over-crowded, you have no prospects for growth options, and you simply must find a way to lovingly decrease attendance. What should you do? The answer is obvious—preach a few messages about giving!

I'm playing, of course, but one dirty little secret of church life is that many people simply stay home if they know the topic is money, and, knowing this, many church leaders don't exactly look forward to this part of our job.

Years ago, our church walked through a giving campaign called *Living Beyond Ourselves*. We were five-years-old as a church and sensed God was moving us beyond our life as a portable community doing church in a movie theater. And, by and large, the response was mind-blowing. For the size of church we were at the time, our people committed significantly more money than the experts told us to expect. This

---

[5] McManus retells the same story in *An Unstoppable Force* (Colorado Springs: David Cook: 2013), p. 320.

confirmed for us that God was indeed moving in our family.

But some people got angry and left.

Asking for money—whether personally to family or friends, or publicly to your church community—isn't easy for us. Yet when we read the Bible, we see again and again that God is not plagued by our uneasiness in this regard.

Probably the most famous example of God asking for money happened in an encounter between Jesus and a certain wealthy young ruler in Mark 10:17-31. This young man was a successful real estate entrepreneur who had amassed many properties. But he was not just a businessman. He was, as we might way, in touch with his spiritual side. He had a deep yearning for God, so he sought Jesus out and asked him how to live a life that pleases God. Jesus said it was simple: just follow God's commands. After Jesus listed a few examples, the young man proudly declared, "I've kept all these since I was a boy!"

Then Jesus looked at him and loved him. The Bible is careful to point out Jesus' love for this man, a love

If we invest our finances in the mission

mysteriously demonstrated in what Jesus said next: "Sell everything you have and give the money to the poor. Then come follow me."

God doesn't hesitate to ask for financial sacrifice.

This example is undoubtedly a bit extreme, but the same basic principle holds true for all scenarios. As part of the Old Testament covenant, God demanded that his people tithe, which meant devoting the first tenth of their earnings to their priests for strictly religious purposes (see Deut 14:22-29. They didn't use cash, so the tithe was made up of animals, crops, and other valuable resources).

And giving is a practice carried forward into New Testament times. Paul, one of the most prominent early church leaders with a penchant for writing letters, tells the churches in Corinth to set aside a certain portion of their income every week so they are prepared to give (1 Cor 16:2). In another letter, he actually commands rich people not to put their hope in wealth, but to be prepared to give whenever they see a need (1 Tim 6:6-10, 17-19).

God doesn't hesitate to ask for money, because it's all

his in the first place. There are no truly self-generated assets, because God made everything that is. At the end of the day, God made you, so, by builder's rights, you and everything you own belong to him.

But God doesn't just say, "Okay, give me back all your money because it's mine in the first place," and walk off gruffly having motivated you to do your religious duty. Not at all! Giving comes with a few promises, in fact. God makes clear what he will do for you if you let go of your precious wealth (even if it's not much).

What he promises is that if we give, a few things will happen. First of all, God will be very happy with us (2 Cor 9:6-7). This has nothing to do with the amount, mind you, but rather with our heart or spirit in giving. One time Jesus watched religious leaders try to out-give one another with large showy financial offerings. Then a poor widow walked forward and gave an amount so small it was almost unnoticeable. Jesus talked during church because he couldn't miss this chance to tell his followers that God was delighted not with the super-pious religious leaders, but with this widow who gave all she had (see Mark 12:41-44).

If we invest our finances in the mission

Second, God is not the only one who will smile brighter when you give. You, too, will also be filled with joy. Maybe not initially, mind you! Parting with our funds can be scary at first, and we sometimes feel dumb for doing it. But over time you find your own heart strangely warmed by the knowledge that you are contributing to the mission of God—that you are "living beyond yourself," as it were.

You very well may also experience blessing financially or materially. I know countless persons and families who have made the oft-difficult decision to start giving or tithing. And though it may have taken a while for them to get used to parting with their funds, before too long they regularly marvel at how God has taken care of their material needs. I have yet to meet someone who started giving regularly and later regretted it. Not one.

But maybe the most significant "blessing" isn't about us at all. It is that other people will benefit from our generosity (see, among others, 2 Cor 9:6-15). The bottom line is that there's someone out there who doesn't know God—who hasn't experienced the life and love that are found only in Christ—who one day

Then our joy will overflow

will come to know these things simply because you chose to give.

Day 2

If we exercise our spiritual gifts
Then the church will strengthen and grow

Anyone who has ever been on a team has likely learned a few lessons about working together. Here are the top five I've learned:

(1) *No one person can do everything.* I think especially of basketball, where the game is such that one all-around great player can be deceived into thinking his teammates are merely ornamental. Kobe had to discover this. Lebron saw this. Even the great Michael Jordan had to learn this.

(2) *If everyone tries to fill the same role, the team will never function as a team.* At a certain point it's not just about being a quality baseball player, but about

becoming a great pitcher or center fielder or second baseman. To stick with baseball, you can't just assemble a lineup of home run hitters and expect to win baseball games. You need pitchers to pitch, hitters to hit, runners to run, and so on.

(3) *Everyone plays a valuable (though not necessarily equal) role.* Everyone from Walt Disney himself down to the folks who keep the grounds clean has played an important role in making Disneyland and Disneyworld uniquely positive experiences. No one would confuse the two, but neither would wise observers deny the value of those who keep things clean.

(4) *You need strength in all roles to be a great team.* You can be a decent acting troupe with a few talented men and women, but in order to be great you've got to have strong people in every role. As the cliché puts it, a team is only as good as its weakest member.

(5) *If anyone down plays the value of another member's role,* overall team morale weakens and performance suffers.

These principles hold true whether your team plays

baseball or sells cookies. You can't ignore them in sports, business, the arts, or family. Or church.

Yes, the same teamwork principles apply to the church—maybe here above all else.

Think about it. No one person can preach sermons, teach kids the Bible, greet new members, make coffee, change diapers, lead worship, and mentor youth—at least not all at the same time! And conversely, not everyone can do any one of these things. Imagine the issues we'd have if everyone showed up on Sunday wanting to teach in the main service, or if every single person wanted to work in the nursery. Related to this, all of these roles—and many more we haven't mentioned—are important. Without them, the church wouldn't function ideally or even smoothly (and we're only talking about weekend services, which is a small part of actually being the church).

It's also true that in order for the church to operate at full capacity, you've got to have good coffee makers make coffee, good diaper-changers changing diapers, good mentors mentoring, friendly folks greeting, and gifted teachers teaching. You can get away with some loose ends here and there, but you'll never be a great church until the right people fill the right spots in the right ways. And finally, if anyone on the team looks down at mates playing other parts, the whole thing starts to fall apart from the middle.

The church is a team, and as such, it needs to remain mindful of all that entails.

Virtually every one of the teamwork rules I mentioned above, and many more besides, are found in 1 Cor 12, where the Apostle Paul talks about how the church must work together to work well.

> *Now to each one the manifestation of the Spirit is given for the common good. To one there is given through the Spirit a message of wisdom, to another a message of knowledge by means of the same Spirit, to another faith by the same Spirit, to another gifts of healing by that one Spirit, to another miraculous powers, to another prophecy, to another distinguishing between spirits, to another speaking in different kinds of tongues, and to still another the interpretation of tongues. All these are the work of one and the*

same Spirit, and he distributes them to each one, just as he determines.

Just as a body, though one, has many parts, but all its many parts form one body, so it is with Christ. For we were all baptized by one Spirit so as to form one body—whether Jews or Gentiles, slave or free—and we were all given the one Spirit to drink. Even so the body is not made up of one part but of many.

Now if the foot should say, "Because I am not a hand, I do not belong to the body," it would not for that reason stop being part of the body. And if the ear should say, "Because I am not an eye, I do not belong to the body," it would not for that reason stop being part of the body. If the whole body were an eye, where would the sense of hearing be? If the whole body were an ear, where would the sense of smell be? But in fact God has placed the parts in the body, every one of them, just as he wanted them to be. If they were all one part, where would the body be? As it is, there are many parts, but one body.

The eye cannot say to the hand, "I don't need

you!" And the head cannot say to the feet, "I don't need you!" On the contrary, those parts of the body that seem to be weaker are indispensable, and the parts that we think are less honorable we treat with special honor. And the parts that are unpresentable are treated with special modesty, while our presentable parts need no special treatment. But God has put the body together, giving greater honor to the parts that lacked it, so that there should be no division in the body, but that its parts should have equal concern for each other. If one part suffers, every part suffers with it; if one part is honored, every part rejoices with it.

Now you are the body of Christ, and each one of you is a part of it. And God has placed in the church first of all apostles, second prophets, third teachers, then miracles, then gifts of healing, of helping, of guidance, and of different kinds of tongues. Are all apostles? Are all prophets? Are all teachers? Do all work miracles? Do all have gifts of healing? Do all speak in tongues? Do all interpret? Now eagerly desire the greater gifts. (1 Cor 12:7-31)

Then the church will strengthen and grow

In other words, we all have a place—a role to play without which the team would suffer. This also means that we all have a responsibility to play that role. Not one of us gets off the hook. We must come to church not only to get, but also to contribute. Not only to receive, but to give as well.

This grates against the consumer mentality we bring with us—well, everywhere. Our culture trains us to think of ourselves as people who are here to be served.

Yet Jesus calls us to the opposite kind of mentality: we join the church to serve rather than consume, to give as much as to receive.

And one of the primary ways we give is, as Paul teaches, by using our gifts to serve the community. Paul's list isn't exhaustive or definitive, mind you. We find other such "gift lists" in Rom 12, Eph 4, and 1 Pet 4. All of these lists together paint a picture of God using what we're good at—or making us good at some things—for the sake of the greater good of all.

So what does all this mean for you? It means you've got to find one of your gifts and start exercising it to build others up.

How do you do that? How do you discover your "spiritual gifts"? It's not a complicated formula really. I'd like to suggest three general guidelines to keep in mind:

(1) *What needs do you see?* What we notice others are doing poorly is often a clue to where we might need to plug in and help—not with some sort of messiah complex or belief that we can save the day, but just making ourselves available for whatever is needed.

(2) *What do you enjoy doing?* What are you passionate about? The next time your church does a volunteer push, just look at the available options and ask, "If I was going to do one of these things, which would I pick?" Then start there. Even if it doesn't work out, at least you've begun the process. Wisdom would suggest that you stick it out for a while, but if after a season of committed service you're just not feeling it, move on to another ministry.

(3) *What have others in the church told you you're good at?* We're notoriously bad at seeing the truth about what we're good at when it comes to serving the church. Sometimes we think we're great at some-

thing, so we give it all we've got only for everyone else to look at each other as if to say, *So, are you gonna tell him he needs a new place to serve, or do I have to?* Other times we think we'd never make a good (fill in the blank), but we do it once as a favor. We thought we stunk, but all everyone else can talk about is how great we were.

It doesn't have to be a conflict though. Sometimes we see a need, think we could do a good job filling it, enjoy ourselves throughout the process, and receive positive feedback from others confirming that we're headed in the right direction.

One key is to release ourselves from the pressure of right now having to find that one place where we can serve with joy. There are likely a number of great options for us, we just need to get going and let God work things out as we walk.

Trial and error is fine. What isn't fine is doing nothing. Or as someone once put it, it's easier to steer a moving vehicle than a parked car. So get going, find a place to serve, and allow God to lead you down a path to fill whatever role he has in mind for you.

Day 3

If we tell people about Jesus
Then God will save others through us

There's a guy who stands on the same street corner almost every day holding up signs that encourage people to accept God's salvation and become followers of Jesus. He's not one of those bombastic types whose signs list all the people God hates. By all appearance, he seems to be a genuinely loving person relaying the good news of God's grace.

But still, I can't help but think that his strategy simply doesn't produce much fruit. In our media message saturated world, it seems that the message of Jesus best breaks into a person's life through a friend or neighbor—through someone they know who can relay the good news over dinner or coffee, rather than through a stranger on a street corner.

Yet whenever I begin feeling critical, I remember a quote from Dwight Moody, one of the most committed and successful twentieth century evangelists. People often criticized his methods for getting the gospel out to people, but his response was simple: "Tell me what you're doing that works and I'll gladly fall in line. But the truth is that you're not doing much. My methods may not be perfect, but I like my methods better than your lack of method."[6]

That's punchy and even insightful, but let's back up and ask the bigger question: In our efforts to spread the gospel, what methods and tactics would be best?

And without doubt, any recipe for the ideal strategy to reach people with the gospel will include two essential ingredients: actions *and* words.

I don't know if you caught it, but the most important word in the last sentence is "and." Actions and words.

One of the most interesting facts about the first few

---

6 James S. Hewett, *Illustrations Unlimited* (Tyndale House Publishers: 1988), p. 178.

centuries of the church's existence is how fast they expanded even though they had no political power, few financial resources, and meager social benefits for those who joined. One early church leader offered his own explanation: *"Beauty of life* encourages strangers to join the ranks. . . . We do not preach great things, but we live them."

People want to see something noteworthy about the way you live before they take interest in what you believe. This isn't rocket science. Actually, it's pretty common sense. There is no way you would consider changing your basic beliefs about reality to align with a group of people you had no desire to imitate. You might never say it this way, but you would want to see the *fruit* of their worldview before you'd even consider internalizing the *root* of it.

So actions are necessary. But actions alone are not enough. Remember the importance of the word "and"—we need actions *and* words. This is something we can never forget.

The hard reality is that words without deeds often do more harm than good. We've all seen this—self-identified "Christians" publicly throwing the Bible at people, only for the rest of us to find out later on that they were hiding some secret scandal or sin. Words without actions often do more harm than good.

But actions without words often do nothing at all.

Truth be told, Tertullian was half-correct. The first Jesus-followers certainly lived beautiful lives. But they also preached a beautiful message. We call this beautiful message the gospel—the good news of what God has done and is doing through Jesus Christ to save the world.

But how can the message be recognized as beautiful if is not understood? And how can it be understood if it is not explained? And how can it be explained if you and I say nothing? How beautiful is the sound of our voices telling others the good news about Jesus!

Yet as great as that may sound, none of us feel like the gospel comes off our lips beautifully. More likely, we stumble our way through seemingly futile attempts to say why we think following Jesus is a great idea.

Well, first of all we need to remember that despite our

feelings, our attempts to tell others about Jesus are hardly futile. God has had no choice but to get quite good at working through imperfect vessels. Or, as one teacher put it, God can draw straight lines with crooked sticks.

But secondly, the Bible gives us some helpful hints and tools for what to say in the moment when actions must become words for Jesus to get his due.

One time, Jesus encountered a demon-possessed man who had essentially been driven crazy by evil spirits. He lived outside the city in tombs, and no one was strong enough to subdue him when he lost his cool. Then Jesus came to town and, long story short, delivered him from his curse. As Jesus was leaving, this man asked to come along, but Jesus strangely refused. Instead, Jesus told him to go home to his family and friends and "tell them how much the Lord has done for you, and how he has had mercy on you" (see Mark 5:1-20).

So that's the first helpful hint: Tell the story of what God has done for you. What was your life like before Jesus, and what has it been like since? Or, if you're a lifetime church member, what would your life look like if you had ever walked away, and what does it look like since you've stayed?

The second hint is tucked away in a letter the Apostle Peter once wrote to Jesus-followers enduring hardship. He tells them to "always be prepared to give an answer to everyone who asks you to give the reason for the hope that you have" (1 Pet 3:15). Helpful hint number two is to be ready to answer the why question—to give reasons for why you believe. You don't have to be a scholar or genius. Just point out what has convinced you that this wild message is actually true. Maybe it's the beauty of creation or how the church has done so much good or the veracity of Jesus' resurrection.

And the third hint is most important: just tell the true story of Jesus. Paul calls this, somewhat poetically, "proclaiming the mystery of Christ" (Col 4:3). You can tell a particular story from the Gospels (biographies of Jesus), or you can tell the Jesus story as a whole—how he came from heaven to earth and suffered a horrible death out of love for us, only to be raised three days later as evidence that God was with him all along.

Then God will save others through us

So there you have it. First, we must live lives worthy of someone noticing. And simultaneously, we are always ready to share our story, give our reasons for faith, or simply tell someone else the truth about Jesus. If we do this—if we testify with our lives as well as our lips—then God will save other people through our witness.

Day 4

If we endure suffering
Then God will reward us eternally

I was sitting in the presence of giants. Oh, they weren't large people—much smaller than me, in fact. But they were giants nonetheless. I was in India with a group of Jesus-followers who had endured persecution from anti-Christian extremists. And they were telling their stories.

One guy was a church-planter in rural India—a man with little more than a moped and a Bible who plants more churches every year than I've worked with in my entire life. He even met a wonderful woman in the process of his ministry, and they began building a life together. One day he and his wife were celebrating at a party with other Christians when his bride became ill. They hopped on the scooter and began making their way through the countryside toward a hospital that had some medicine she needed. But along the way, he noticed a number of masked men on motorcycles crowding around them. He sped up as fast as he could, but their bikes were faster so they caught up and knocked him and his wife off their scooter with a metal pole. One moment, he was being beaten all over his body. The next moment, he woke up in a hospital to find out that his beautiful young wife didn't survive the attack.

Through tears of sadness he professed his love for Christ, and assured us that no matter how much he lost, he would never stop preaching the good news of Jesus.

We saw the same faith in a preacher who had grown up as the son and grandson of leaders of a large tribe of folks. He himself was next in line to lead. During his teenage years, he made some unwise decisions, and after bailing him out of jail, his father took him before the entire tribe (thousands and thousands of people), and publicly disowned him. "This boy has done some terrible things," he said. "He is no longer my son. I don't know this young man." And they all left. The young man became suicidal before being rescued by Christ. He later became a pastor, and instead of serving in new territory where he hadn't been so humiliated and publicly shamed, he went back to the very tribe and family that kicked him onto the street.

We also heard from a woman whose husband was a pastor. Six months prior, extremists attacked their village, hunting down Christians and especially ministers. Right in front of her, they demanded that her husband denounce Christ so he could live. He refused. So they doused him with kerosene and lit him on fire. This woman watched her husband burn alive.

She could not contain her tears, but she still wasn't considering walking away from the God for whose sake she had undergone suffering beyond what you or I could imagine.

Remaining in Jesus is easy so long as life stays relatively pain-free. Sometimes life is hard. Even worse, sometimes life gets hard because of our commitment to Jesus.

Question: What do you say to someone who has lost everything and yet still believes?

Answer: Nothing.

You'd be a fool to speak, because their lives have already said enough.

Faith like this brings Paul's words to light:

> *Therefore we do not lose heart. Though outwardly we are wasting away, yet inwardly we are being renewed day by day. For our light and momentary troubles are achieving for us an eternal glory that far outweighs them all. So we fix our eyes not on what is seen, but what is unseen, since what is seen is temporary, but what is unseen is eternal. (2 Cor 4:16-18)*

Question: What investment could possibly be worth losing your life?

Answer: One that can only be measured against eternity.

The Apostle Paul wrote many letters, but the last one is what we call 2 Timothy. He wrote this letter to

Timothy, whom he had loved and mentored for decades. Paul had given Timothy a difficult assignment and Timothy was struggling to remain faithful to his task, so Paul wrote to encourage his young friend to stay the course.

Tucked away in 2 Timothy is a promise Paul offers anyone in a season of suffering: *If we endure, we will also reign with him* (2 Tim 2:12).

In this book we've covered a lot of "ifs" and "thens," haven't we? We began by talking about the promise that if we surrender our lives to God, he will save us in every way. God stands always ready to save, for he is our Savior, and all we need to do is receive the gift he offers. Then we learned that if we seek God, God promises that we will find him. We will discover that God was seeking us all along and promises to bring us into an active relationship with him. After that, we unpacked what it means to remain in Jesus and see God's Spirit produce the fruit of God's life in and through us. Then in week four we looked at some matters of obedience, where God promises that if we just do things his way, then we will be blessed. And this week we've looked at different aspects of serving God—with our money, with our gifts, with our actions and words—and learning how God multiplies our small investments to make a big impact.

But here at the end we need to cover this one final if/then, which is not so much about a certain kind of obedience or investment, but rather the degree or extent of both. If we follow beyond the point of obvious payback, what then? What could be worth suffering, even death? The Bible answers this question with the ultimate guarantee: eternal life. It may sound crazy, but God promises that we will live together in a new creation enjoying the direct presence of God and the company of all his people.

The equation is simple: *if you invest your life, then you get back eternity.*

Or to quote Paul again in one of the greatest if/then statements in all of Scripture,

> *Now he has reconciled you by Christ's physical body through death to present you holy in his sight, without blemish and free from accusation—if you continue in your faith, established and firm, and do not move from the hope held*

out in the gospel. This is the gospel that you heard and that has been proclaimed to every creature under heaven. (Col 1:22-23)

Epilogue

My family loves to go to amusement parks. Our girls are at such an age that they love it and don't mind walking hand and hand with their parents. So we hit all the rides they are tall enough to ride. Not long ago, we visited Six Flags Magic Mountain and we learned that Sidney, our youngest, was now tall enough to ride Goliath. For those of you unaware, Goliath is an amazing ride of epic proportions. It has a 255-foot drop and travels up to eighty-five miles an hour. It's been known to make some people black out through some of the turns. We decided we needed to ride it.

As we approached, our seven-year-old Sidney began to get cold feet. "I don't want to ride it," she said. This would require someone to sit out with her. But you have to understand, in our family we have a principle—it's not a biblical principle, just a principle: everyone rides. No one was waiting around with Sid while the rest of us rode. We were all going to ride!

If/Then

So what began as a family of four happily bounding toward a fun roller coaster quickly became three people dragging a crying child to what she believed would be her impending death. We did our best to hide her tears; after all, we didn't want to cause a scene. I put her in the car with me, tried to help her think happy thoughts, and finally the ride began. The climb up the hill seemed to take forever. She clutched my hand like her life depended on it. And then . . . the drop. Eighty-five miles an hour down 255 feet into a tunnel of darkness and screams, but as we emerged I looked over only to see a huge smile on her face. As the ride came to an end she screamed, "Let's ride it again!" And we did. Four more times. Until dad was the one crying.

This experience reminded me of what it is like to follow God. It all looks great till we see the size of the challenge and the speed at which change can sometimes come. Seeking God first, dying to self, pursuing his kingdom instead of ours—these all can seem like daunting tasks that can bring all of us to a state of fear. We think, *If this is what it means to participate in God's wonderful plan for my life, count*

Epilogue

me out! But when we sit it out, we miss the thrill of the ride.

We are blessed to have a Heavenly Father who has not left us alone to chase him, nor has he dogged behind to correct us. He wants to work with us to become the people he created us to be. And just like a roller coaster, there are highs, there are lows, there are moments of darkness, and moments of sunlight. But we are never alone. Our Father holds our hand and leads us through. This is our life with God. Don't sit this one out.

Acknowledgments

Acknowledgments from Rusty:

I'm so thankful for Leadership Network and their invitation for me to become part of one of their Senior Leader groups. It was there that I met Mike Lee and had this If/Then principle cemented in my mind. I'm also grateful for the wonderful friendship and collaboration I've experienced with Michael DeFazio over the last eight years. I never knew I could feel like a big brother and a kid brother with the same person. Your encouragement, wisdom and passion have been a blessing to me.

Thank you to Mark Mears and Fred Gray for forcing this book to happen and for all your belief in us. And thank you to the Board of Directors of Real Life Church who trust me and love me and give me the job of a lifetime.

Special thanks to my wife Lorrie who brings so much

joy and laughter and beauty to my life. And to our girls Lindsey and Sidney... I'm grateful for the stories you provide, but more grateful for the life you bring to our family.

Acknowledgments from Michael:

It has become cliche to acknowledge that book writing is never a solitary endeavor, but I'm happy that in this case it's neither cliche nor metaphor. I owe my first thanks to Rusty for not only sharing with me the If/Then concept, but also inviting me to help bring the book to fruition. While we have collaborated mostly over long distances, writing alongside him has reminded me of all the ways God has used him in my life as a mentor and friend. Without him I probably wouldn't make much sense.

I mostly wrote my portions while still on staff at Real Life Church, so pride of place must also go to my team there. Special thanks to Fred Gray and Brennan Conklin for always being fantastic sounding boards (among other things!). And to Jason VanderPal for staying on top of how this book will actually serve the church in our Life Groups as we eat, learn, serve, and play together.

Just as the actual publishing process began I moved away, so I'm sure more people helped carry this book across the 'finish' line than I am aware of. I do know that serious contributions came from Mark Mears and Daniel Furukawa, for which I am very grateful. And as always, it was a joy to work with Caleb Seeling and his team at Samizdat Creative to help bring our words to life.

Lastly, of course, I am grateful for my wife Beth. I don't even like to think about the then that would follow if she had not accepted the invitation to become my bride. If we live another ten or twenty or fifty years together, then by that time I may have more joy than I know what to do with.

About the Authors

RUSTY GEORGE, Lead Pastor
Real Life Church, California

Rusty George is the Lead Pastor of Real Life Church in Santa Clarita, California, which Outreach Magazine 2011 named one of the fastest growing churches in America. Rusty's story did not begin in California, however. He hails from the Midwest. Born in Oklahoma, Rusty spent his childhood in Wichita, Kansas, and after high school, Rusty attended Ozark Christian College in Joplin, Missouri, where his Youth Pastor had gone before him. Rusty had known since age 13 that he wanted to be in ministry. He thought he'd be a youth pastor, too, but God had other plans.

A huge fan of the L.A. Lakers, Rusty spent four years of college on the Ozark basketball team, and earned a double major—a B.A. in Biblical Studies and a B.A. in Preaching. Before his junior year, Rusty met Lorrie Miller. The couple dated for two years and wed in 1994—the same month they both graduated from Ozark.

During the last two summers of Rusty's college career, he served as an intern with Southland Christian Church in Lexington, Kentucky. Upon his graduation, Southland offered Rusty a full-time job as the College Pastor. Rusty spent the next nine years at Southland, moving from College Pastor to Young Adult Pastor and finally to Age Level Director, all while attending Cincinnati Christian Seminary. At that point, Rusty knew God was moving in his heart to do something different. He considered joining with a few friends to plant a church in an unchurched area of North Carolina.

But again, God had other plans. Instead, Rusty received a call from his colleague and friend, Kyle Idleman, who was then Lead Pastor and founder of

Real Life Church in Valencia. Kyle, too, was feeling called to another church, and had recommended to RLC's Board that Rusty take his position at Real Life. After a few meetings and trips to California, Rusty and Lorrie took the plunge, moved to California, and accepted the position of Lead Pastor of Real Life Church in 2003.

The California culture was a change for the Georges, but it quickly became home, and they began a family. Daughter Lindsey was born in 2002, and Sidney was born in 2004. Rusty has led RLC through many changes, including the purchase of land, the construction of an eco-friendly building in the middle of town, and the incredible growth of meeting in a 285-seat movie theater at the mall, to a high school gym, now to two campuses where more than 5,500 people attend services each week. Through all the changes, Rusty's vision for Real Life Church has remained the blueprint for its growth: to be a church that unchurched people find irresistible in its mission of helping people find and follow Jesus.

MICHAEL DEFAZIO

Professor of New Testament and Hermeneutics

Ozark Christian College

Michael is a Professor of New Testament and Hermeneutics at Ozark Christian College in Joplin, Missouri. (Which is a fancy way of saying he teaches the Bible and how to study the Bible.) He grew up down the road in Tulsa, Oklahoma, in a large, loving, loud Italian family. On the advice of his pastors and in the steps of his older sister, Michael attended Ozark where he earned a Bachelor of Theology in New Testament. While at Ozark he helped lead the small groups ministry of a local church as well as preaching pastor at a small congregation in rural Missouri.

Also while at Ozark he met a beautiful and wonderfully gifted woman named Beth, who in 2003 would become his wife. After college they had secure plans to move to Kentucky, but just a few weeks before graduation he got a call from Rusty asking about the possibility of heading his way instead. After a (short!) time of praying and visiting, they decided God was leading them to the coast and headed west.

Michael served eight years on staff at Real Life Church, working in various adult ministry capacities such as teaching and overseeing the Life Groups team. He attended Fuller Theological Seminary where he earned a M.A. in Theology with an emphasis on Biblical Studies and Theology. Michael and Beth also had their two children while in California—Claire (May 2010) and Carson (April 2013). Right about the time he decided their family would likely stay at Real Life for another long while, he unexpectedly got a call from Ozark. Much as he hated to go, this was the one thing he'd long thought about leaving to do.

More than anything else, Michael wants to help people wrestle with who Jesus is and what it means to follow him today. In Spring 2011 he wrote *Jesus in 3D*, which is a popular-level introduction to the life and teachings of Jesus. In the book, Michael answers such questions as: What story does Jesus fulfill? What did Jesus come here to do? Why did Jesus die? and What difference does Jesus' resurrection make? And in fall 2012 he wrote *moreJESUS*, which takes readers on a six-week journey through Paul's letter to the Colossians.

About Real Life Church

Located in Southern California, Real Life Church is a non-denominational Christian church committed to its Mission: Helping People Find and Follow Jesus. The church represents one "body" that meets together through three connected campuses: Valencia, Newhall @ Savia and Online (online.reallifechurch.org).

As its name suggests, each Real Life Church campus provides a diverse array of programs, worship styles, ministries and pastoral care opportunities that serve as a 'bridge' between the Real Life issues we all face as fallible human beings and the promise of Real Life that God has planned for each one of us.

Founded in 2000 as a church plant from Shepherd of the Hills in Porter Ranch, Real Life Church strives to serve as the "hands and feet of Jesus" by providing all people with a message of hope and healing -- no matter who they are, where they come from or what season of life in which they may find themselves.

Heeding its own call to multiply, Real Life Church planted Mission Church in Ventura in 2011.

For more information about Real Life Church, or to participate in a weekend service either in person or via its Online campus, please go to www.reallifechurch.org.

CPSIA information can be obtained at www.ICGtesting.com
Printed in the USA
LVOW07*0718300813

349921LV00002B/2/P